Oklahoma

OKLAHOMA BY ROAD

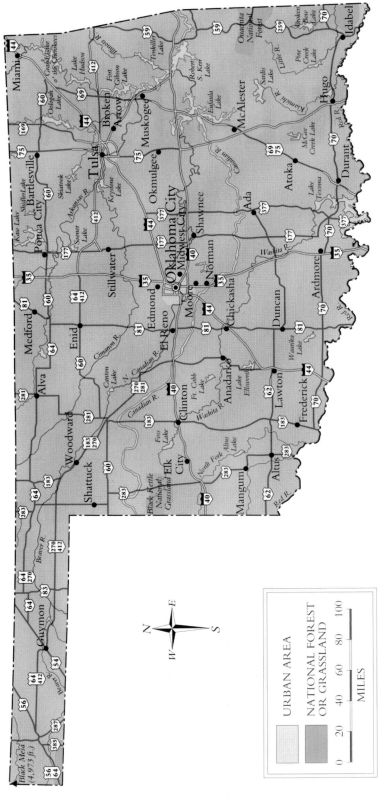

Celebrate the States

Oklahoma

Guy Baldwin and Joyce Hart

mc Marshall Cavendish
Benchmark
New York

Marshall Cavendish Benchmark
99 White Plains Road
Tarrytown, NY 10591-5502
www.marshallcavendish.us

All Internet addresses were correct and accurate at the time of printing.

Library of Congress Cataloging-in-Publication Data
Baldwin, Guy.
Oklahoma / by Guy Baldwin and Joyce Hart.—2nd ed.
p. cm. — (Celebrate the states)
Summary: "Provides comprehensive information on the geography, history, wildlife, governmental
structure, economy, cultural diversity, peoples, religion, and landmarks of
Oklahoma"—Provided by publisher.
Includes bibliographical references and index.
ISBN 978-0-7614-4032-1
1. Oklahoma—Juvenile literature. I. Hart, Joyce. II. Title.

F694.3.B36 2010
976.6—dc22
2008044261

Editor: Christine Florie
Co-Editor: Denise Pangia
Publisher: Michelle Bisson
Art Director: Anahid Hamparian
Series Designer: Adam Mietlowski

Photo research and layout by Marshall Cavendish International (Asia) Private Limited—
Thomas Khoo, Benson Tan and Shawn Wee

Cover photo by Corbis

The photographs in this book are used by permission and through the courtesy of, *Lonely Planet Images*: back cover, 56, 62, 67, 89, 90, 94, 96, 104, 116, 130, 131, 133, 135, 137; *Photolibrary*: 8, 11, 12, 18, 21, 22, 42, 53, 58, 66, 68, 77, 87, 98, 107, 111, 115, 129, 132; *Corbis*: 10, 25, 45, 49, 54, 75, 92, 97, 99, 117, 123, 126, 134, 136; *Getty Images*: 13, 24, 47, 71, 78, 81, 85, 88, 119, 120, 124, 125, 127, 128; *Photolibrary / Alamy*: 16, 26, 30, 32, 35, 38, 51, 101, 105; *North Wind Picture Archives*: 28, *Naional Geographic Society Image Collection*: 83.

Printed in Malaysia
1 3 5 6 4 2

Contents

Oklahoma Is . . .

. . . a place where people want to live.

"It is a place for people who have 'an attitude that all things are possible if people are willing to take a chance and embrace the future without hesitation or reservation.'"

—journalist Angelo Scott

We know we belong to the land
And the land we belong to is grand!
And when we say
Yeeow! Ayipioeeay!
We're only sayin'
You're doin' fine, Oklahoma!

—lyrics by Oscar Hammerstein II for the musical *Oklahoma!*,
with music by Richard Rodgers

"We were there. High up the trees flurried with birdsong, and one clear note sang above the rest, a lucid, soaring strand of sound; . . . I breathed deeply the blossoms and sunlight and there was a sigh in it. I thought, Here is the place to stay, grow up with the state, take root."

—novelist Ralph Ellison, *Juneteenth*

"I want my permanent address to be in Oklahoma . . . that's where I want to raise my kids."

—singer/songwriter Carrie Underwood

Oklahoma is expansive . . .

"Oklahoma is tallgrass prairie and everlasting mountains. It is secret patches of ancient earth tromped smooth and hard by generations of dancing feet. It is the cycle of song and heroic deed. It is calloused hands. It is the aroma of rich crude oil fused with the scent of sweat and sacred smoke."

—writer Michael Wallis

Oklahoma has a rich, contradictory history.

"It is difficult to set down the solemn facts about Oklahoma without their reading like something copied out of an insane encyclopedia."

—writer George Milburn

Its people deal stoutheartedly with hard conditions.

"No question about it. We take it on the chin, but we don't give in."

—television meteorologist Gary England

"Resilience is woven deeply into the fabric of Oklahoma. Throw us an obstacle, and we grow stronger."

—Oklahoma governor Brad Henry

Oklahoma is a land of great variety, both in its landscape and in its people. From its rocky mountains to its steep valleys, from marshy wetlands to dusty deserts, from the hundreds of lakes to some of the largest fields of grassy prairie land, Oklahoma is unique. The state was once called Indian Territory and today remains home to one of the largest American-Indian populations in the United States. Oklahoma also has a rich history of successful African-American towns that thrived while other states struggled with the issue of freed slaves. This is a land of cowboys and oil rigs, prairie dogs and vast fields of gypsum that brightly reflect the sun like glass. In all of Oklahoma's variety, it is an interesting state to visit and an exciting state to call home.

Chapter One

Wild Open Spaces

On the map Oklahoma resembles a jagged butcher's cleaver with the strip in the northwest as its handle and the wiggly line to the south—the Red River—as its cutting edge. The state also shares borders with New Mexico to the west, Kansas and Colorado to the north, Missouri and Arkansas to the east, and Texas, south and west. The state's widest point, east to west across the northern border, measures 478 miles (770 kilometers). North to south, along the eastern border, Oklahoma runs 231 miles (370 km). Overall, Oklahoma claims 69,903 square miles (181 square km), making it the twentieth largest state. It is a beautiful state with a varied landscape of forests, mountains, and flat open plains.

Oklahoma's borders enclose a rich mixture of landscapes. In both the northeastern edges and the southern portion, mountains border the state. As you travel across the state, Oklahoma offers a welcoming variety of plateaus, plains, and hills.

MOUNTAINS AND A HIGH PLATEAU

Forested foothills and low mountains shape northeastern Oklahoma, where the Ozark Plateau stands with its tall pines and twisting steep-

Oklahoma's landscape varies from green, flat grasslands to dry, rocky hillsides.

9

walled valleys. In this northeastern corner are the cities of Miami, Vinita, and Grove.

In the southeastern corner, along the border with Arkansas, the Ouachita Mountains rise. The Ouachita range is a mass of narrow slabs of yellow sandstone that have been pushed up and set on their sides by geological pressures over vast time. These peaks are cloaked in forests of loblolly pine and cedar and are dotted with spring-fed lakes. There are no big cities in this

High cliffs, dotted with pine trees, make ideal lookouts for hawks and eagles.

area. Small towns like Hugo and Poteau populate this part of the state. Here, too, is part of the Ouachita National Forest, one of the largest and oldest national forests in the southern portion of the United States.

The rougher and more rugged Arbuckle and Wichita ranges are found in south central and southwestern Oklahoma. Volcanic pressure pushing up from deep inside the earth caused these granite peaks to rise. Actually, only the peaks of these mountains are visible. Geologist Charles Gould wrote that the Wichitas are "nothing but the tops of buried mountain ranges projecting above and surrounded by a sea of plain." The cities of Ada and Pauls Valley are not too far from this area. Mostly this is a great land for outdoor recreation, with big campgrounds such as the ones developed in Chickasaw National Recreation Area.

These huge boulders on the slope of Mount Scott in Wichita Mountains Wildlife Refuge show signs of seasonal water erosion.

HILLS AND PLAINS

Moving east to west across the rest of the state, Oklahoma is cut into wide and varying bands of land forms. There are the Prairie Plains, the Sandstone Hills, the Red Beds Plains, the Gypsum Hills, and finally, leading into the panhandle part of the state, the High Plains.

The plains, in general, often seem flat at first glance, but a closer look reveals sudden woodlands, hidden gullies, and abrupt swells of exposed rock. Of the Oklahoma plains, journalist Phil Brown wrote, "We can see from horizon to horizon with the exception of the forests of blackjack trees growing so closely together that it looks as if it would be difficult to walk through them."

These fertile plains, such as the Prairie Plains and the Red Beds Plains, eventually blend into the higher, harsher High Plains of the northwest section of the state, into the Panhandle—the narrow strip of

Typical summer days in Oklahoma are hot and dry in the Panhandle.

land at top that juts west from the rest of the state. Found there are gray gypsum and red sandstone that peek through the thin soil and rivers that cut wavy scratches across the land. It is in the High Plains region that the highest point in the state, Black Mesa, at 4,973 feet (1,515 meters), is located. Cottonwood, willow, and tamarisk trees huddle in the river lowlands. Higher up, prairie grasses cover much of the plains. This landscape "has a thorny personality," said Oklahoma geologist Gary Thompson. Its plants and animals are "designed to puncture, penetrate, and poison"—from diamondback rattlesnakes and horned toads to prickly pear cactus, burrs, and spiky thickets of wild plums.

Oklahoma's arid landscapes provide perfect environments for diamondback rattlesnakes.

Cutting across the plains are the Sandstone Hills and Gypsum Hills regions. It was in the Sandstone Hills lands that oil was first found in Oklahoma. The Sandstone Hills lie in the center of the state and run north to south. The elevation of these hills runs from about 250 to 400 feet (75 to 120 m). Tulsa, the state's second largest city, is located there, and is home to Holmes Peak, which stands at 1,030 feet (315 m). Much of the rest of the Sandstone Hills region is scattered with oil wells that have run dry and deserted small towns that sprang up around them.

The Gypsum Hills area is found west of the Red Beds Plains. These hills, which are at most 200 feet (60 m) high, are lower than the Sandstone Hills. Large deposits of gypsum, which in a powdered form is made into chalk and plaster of paris, are found in this area. Oklahoma is one of the biggest suppliers of gypsum in the United States. A large amount is produced in the city of Bessie. One of the world's largest single deposits of pure alabaster, a form of gypsum, is found in the Alabaster Caverns State Park near Freedom.

WATERWAYS

Oklahoma has hundreds of rivers and creeks, but two really stand out: the Red River, which meanders along the state's southern border, and the Arkansas River in the northeast, which is an important shipping lane. Since dams, dredging, and channel widening were completed in 1970, the Arkansas River Navigation System, called the McClellan-Kerr Arkansas River Navigation System (MKARNS), has opened river routes to shipping traffic from the Mississippi River as far west as Tulsa. Ships can sail to Tulsa's Port of Catoosa from any ocean in the world, making it one of America's most important inland ports.

Although Oklahoma's eastern rivers tend to flow deeply through well-defined channels, its western rivers and streams behave quite differently. They flow more irregularly and carry far more sand, clay, and gravel. As the water cuts a channel, these materials fill the river channels back in again. The result is wide, shallow, muddy rivers such as the Cimarron, Canadian, and Washita rivers, which can spill from one channel to another when there is a lot of water. Those murky rivers tend to dry up completely when rainfall is low.

WHERE'S THE BORDER?

The wriggling, muddy, disorderly Red River forms the southern border of Oklahoma. Where the land is flat, the river often changes course, jumping its bank to carve new channels. Every time this happens, part of Texas becomes part of Oklahoma, or the other way around.

This stretch of river has been baffling border makers for centuries. Spain and the United States argued about it when the United States acquired the area north of the river in 1803. During the 1920s Texas Rangers and the Oklahoma National Guard nearly clashed over the issue. Tax collectors, law enforcement officials, and wildlife managers in both Oklahoma and Texas scratched their heads every time the river moved, wondering who was responsible for the nearby land.

The two states studied the problem for years. In 1999 they at last agreed that the boundary should be on the south bank of the river along the "vegetation line," where trees and bushes have grown along the river's usual path. "It solves problems that have plagued citizens of the Red River Valley for almost 200 years," said Bill Abney, a Texan who helped negotiate the solution. The Red River still wanders. But now when it shifts course, the two states know what to do about it—though they may have to wait a few years to see just where the new vegetation line grows.

Oklahoma has more than one hundred natural lakes, but humans have made even more. The state has about two hundred man-made lakes. Together these lakes give Oklahoma more than one million surface-acres of water. Dams and diversions have created two hundred artificial lakes in the state—partly for recreation, though also to control flooding and to supply hydroelectric power. One of the largest fabricated lakes in Oklahoma is Lake Eufaula, whose clear waters attract boaters and anglers.

Dams along many of Oklahoma's rivers provide electricity, as well as water recreation.

LAND AND WATER

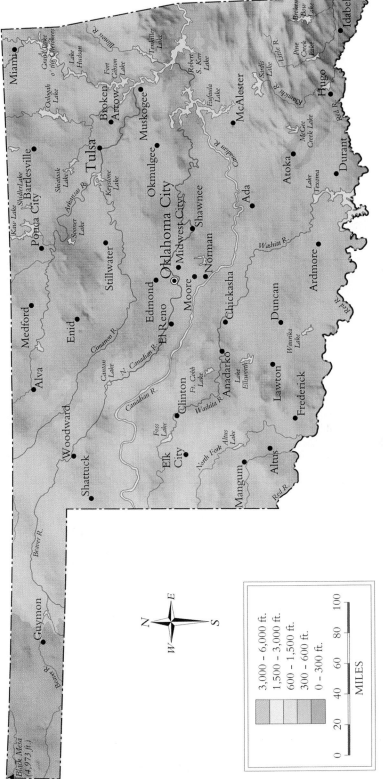

Miami

Grand Lake o' the Cherokees

Lake Hudson

Illinois R.

Tenkiller Lake

Broken Bow Lake

Idabel

Pine Creek Lake

Little R.

Hugo

Red R.

Sardis Lake

Kiamichi R.

McAlester

Robert S. Kerr Lake

Fort Gibson Lake

Oologah Lake

Broken Arrow

Muskogee

Eufaula Lake

McGee Creek Lake

Durant

Bartlesville

Tulsa

Skiatook Lake

Keystone Lake

Okmulgee

Atoka

Lake Texoma

Kaw Lake

Shidler Lake

Ponca City

Arkansas R.

Sooner Lake

Canadian R.

Ada

Shawnee

Oklahoma City

Midwest City

Norman

Washita R.

Ardmore

Stillwater

Medford

Enid

Edmond

El Reno

Moore

Chickasha

Duncan

Waurika Lake

Cimarron R.

Alva

Canton Lake

N. Canadian R.

Ft. Cobb Lake

Anadarko

Lake Ellsworth

Lawton

Frederick

Red R.

Woodward

Clinton

Washita R.

Canadian R.

Foss Lake

Elk City

North Fork Altus Lake

Mangum

Altus

Red R.

Shattuck

Beaver R.

Guymon

Beaver R.

Black Mesa (4,973 ft.)

N E S W

MILES

3,000 – 6,000 ft.
1,500 – 3,000 ft.
600 – 1,500 ft.
300 – 600 ft.
0 – 300 ft.

0   20   40   60   80   100

A LIVELY LANDSCAPE

Oklahoma's varied landscape provides homes for a wide range of plants and animals. Deer, moose, elk, and antelope freely roam prairie lands; bears and coyotes can also be found. The state's smaller animals include armadillos, opossums, and rabbits.

Oklahoma is home to a variety of animals, such as this armadillo.

UNDERDOGS OF THE PLAINS

Not long ago, Oklahoma's prairie lands featured vast prairie dog towns—fields speckled with openings to an underground network of tunnels and dens, created and tended by cute but ferocious little rodents. "They can bite through welder's gloves," said wildlife expert Rebecca Fischer. "Their giant incisors [front teeth] are like little chisels."

Ranchers often despise prairie dogs for eating the grass, chewing fence posts, and digging holes that become hazardous for horses whose legs can shatter with a misstep into one of the holes. Trapping, shooting, and poisoning the prairie dogs, as well as naturally occurring diseases and housing and business developments, at one time had wiped out 99 percent of the unwanted creatures nationwide. In 1998 the black-tailed prairie dog was placed on a threatened species list. The endangered label never came, though. In 2004 they were even removed from the "to be considered" list.

Today prairie dog populations are increasing slightly in Oklahoma, though only a very small percent of the original density remains. In the meantime, scientists have discovered that prairie dogs actually support plants and other animals in the prairie ecosystem. Because of the prairie dogs' digging, weedy plants that are high in nutrition are thriving. These plants help to support the needs of grazing animals such as cattle, bison, antelope, and elk.

Naturalists are helping to reestablish prairie dog towns in places like the Martin Park Nature Center in Oklahoma City. A prairie dog town defends itself by constant vigilance. Some of the animals work as lookouts—individual prairie dogs stand on top of hills, peering about and sniffing the air for signs of danger. When one spies trouble, it spreads the alarm, and all the other prairie dogs duck for cover into their maze of holes and tunnels. Unfortunately, all their security vigilance has not been enough to save them.

Oklahoma's lakes and streams support catfish, bass, perch, sunfish, and trout. Many different birds also call Oklahoma home. These include the roadrunner and the scissor-tailed flycatcher, Oklahoma's state bird.

Near the northwestern town of Freedom, plumes of what look like dark, sooty smoke rise at sunset on the horizon during summer. At daybreak, the same occurs in reverse, as if the earth were sucking the smoke back in. But it is not smoke. It is thick clouds of bats, about a million of them. They belong to one of the largest bat colonies in the United States, the Selman Bat Cave. They sleep in caves by day and rise at night to hunt, eating almost 10 tons of insects every night. These busy mammals migrate to Mexico in winter. Bat viewing events are held at the caves during the summer.

Before farmers and homesteaders moved to Oklahoma, much of the state was covered with native prairie grasses, the tallest of it growing where the most rain fell. But farmers plowed under most of the grasses. The Tallgrass Prairie Preserve north of Pawhuska is one of the last remaining large sections of this magnificent windswept grassland. Vast herds of bison used to live on this grassland before they were hunted to the brink of extinction in the nineteenth century. A new bison herd, established in the early 1990s, is helping to restore the original ecology of this area.

Visitors to Oklahoma will notice what look like big, messy birds' nests in the branches of many trees. A closer look reveals the state flower—mistletoe, which grows as a parasite on trees. The state is a major supplier of the mistletoe sprigs that are so popular during the winter holidays.

At dusk, Mexican freetail bats stream across Oklahoma skies in search of dinner.

WILD WEATHER

Oklahoma is well known for its diverse and violent weather. Every spring, tornadoes sweep the state, causing people to dive for the safety of their basements or storm shelters. Damage to buildings is often enormous. "I've always wanted skylights," joked Marian Keef after a twister ripped the roof off her bedroom. Her husband, Ron, put the damage in perspective: "We've got nothing to gripe about. We're alive, and we're not hurt."

Oklahomans experience some of the country's most dramatic weather, including powerful tornadoes.

They were lucky. Some of the worst tornadoes in memory hit central Oklahoma in the spring of 1999, including one near Mulhall that appeared to be a mile wide. In a matter of minutes, a thousand houses near Oklahoma City were flattened. More than forty people died and 675 were injured. On March 31, 2004, Oklahoma City was hit by two tornadoes in the same day.

Because of its severe weather, Oklahoma is home to the National Severe Storms Laboratory and the Storm Prediction Center, which have helped turn the art of storm forecasting into a science. Gary England, a popular television meteorologist, remembered when the only clue that a tornado was approaching was when "it blew down your friend's house up the road." Now, sophisticated equipment like Doppler radar helps England get the word out about dangerous weather fast enough to save lives.

Another weather hazard is drought. In recent years many farmers have lost their crops because of low rainfall. Rancher Truman Zybach had to sell his cattle because he couldn't feed them. "We're plum out of green grass," he lamented. All across Oklahoma the fields baked dry. Farmers squinted at fields of bare, parched soil. "We probably haven't seen in most of our lifetimes a drought this severe," reflected Pat McDowell of the Oklahoma Agriculture Department. According to the 2008 U.S. Drought Monitor, all of the western portion of the state as well as most of the northern part was listed as "abnormally dry" to moderate drought. The panhandle area is suffering through its most severe drought in decades. The 2008 season was the second driest on record, even drier than in the ruinous Dust Bowl days of the 1930s.

THE DUST BOWL

Real old-timers in Oklahoma remember the terrible droughts of the 1930s—the legendary Dust Bowl years, which lasted, in some parts, for the entire decade. Some days, great storms of dust darkened the skies, blotting out the sun. In the midst of a storm (as shown below), the air might be so thick with dust that people had to cover their faces even while they slept so they would not breathe in the powdery soil that blew through the screens on their windows.

The disaster was in part caused by farmers plowing away the hardy, drought-resistant prairie grasses and replacing them with wheat and cotton. When the drought hit, the farmers' crops died and left the fine soil exposed to wind and water erosion. The soil became so dry that during a series of drought years much of western Oklahoma's topsoil blew away. It was one of the worst environmental disasters in U.S. history. One particular day, April 14, 1935, has been called Black Sunday, because huge thick dust storms swept across the plains that day.

Because of the drought and the dust storms, huge numbers of farming families were forced to leave their land behind. Many migrated to California. These migrants were given the name Okies, because so many of them came from Oklahoma. John Steinbeck, a famous American author, brought attention to the plight of these displaced Oklahoma Dust Bowl families in his powerful novel *The Grapes of Wrath*, later (1940) made into a movie with Henry Fonda and Jane Darwell.

Despite the droughts that are common in the state, farmers have learned different methods to farm their land.

Droughts are a natural condition in the state. Oklahoma is positioned on the edge of an arid zone, where absence of rain is a natural condition. Today dry years still mean the loss of the fertile topsoil and the failure of crops, but farmers have learned to lessen this loss by plowing along the contours of the land and by rotating what they plant so that a single crop doesn't wear out the soil. Like all Oklahomans, they've come to appreciate their land's ornery personality. More than ever, they strive to adapt to the land—rather than the other way around.

Chapter Two

Indian Territory to State

"Although it was one of the last of the states to enter the Union, Oklahoma has in one sense the most unusual history of them all," remarked historian Lawrence Goodwyn. The flags of Spain, France, Mexico, the Republic of Texas, and the Confederate States of America have flown there. Many American-Indian tribes have followed different trails to this land. The making of the state of Oklahoma contrasts get-rich-quick stories of land rushes and oil booms with the hardscrabble lives of sharecroppers and the disaster of the Dust Bowl tragedy. Mixed through all these accounts are countless stories of ordinary people building lives and communities in what would become the state of Oklahoma.

EARLY TIMES

Recorded history covers only the tiniest part of human experience in what would become Oklahoma. People began living on this land at least

The first land rush of Oklahoma began on April 22, 1889, where thousands of settlers raced from the eastern border to stake a piece of unclaimed land.

15,000 years ago. They were nomadic tribes who moved from place to place, following game and gathering wild plants. Scientists have classified those people by the names Clovis and Folsom cultures. Those who study these early cultures have distinguished between them by the different types of arrowheads that have been found and dated. These earliest people lived in caves and on the rocky ledges of bluffs and sides of mountains. Others lived along the riverbanks, where access to food and a means of transportation were available. There are also signs that somewhere around 4000 B.C.E., some tribes started building settlements. Their houses were built of mud and grass.

About 2,500 years ago a group of ancient people settled down and raised crops on present-day Oklahoma land. Scientists have found the ruins of villages that were strewn with animal bones and stone tools. Remnants of fields, where corn, beans, and squash had once grown, were also discovered. Spiro Mounds, in eastern Oklahoma close to the Arkansas border, seems to have been an important political and religious center for the newly settled tribes. The people who lived there have been named Mound Builders, and they belonged to a system of communities that traded with other tribes as far away as the Great Lakes and the Pacific Ocean. Spiro was abandoned before 1450 for reasons that remain unclear.

Ruins of Mound Builders' villages were discovered by scientists several thousands of years ago.

SPIRO MOUNDS ARCHAEOLOGICAL PARK

Spiro Mounds is Oklahoma's only archaeological park. Scientists are studying a 150-acre (61-ha) site there that includes twelve earthen mounds, evidence that an ancient culture lived on that site from about 850 C.E. until 1450 C.E. Because of the large number of artifacts that archaeologists have found there, Spiro Mounds is considered one of the most important prehistoric Indian sites east of the Rocky Mountains. Scientists have concluded that Spiro must have been a center of commerce for the ancient tribal people. They have also surmised that the mounds were places of religious or spiritual ceremonies. The mounds were also places of burial for the most revered leaders of the tribes.

The first written record of what would become Oklahoma dates to 1541, when the Spanish explorer Francisco Vásquez de Coronado led an army across the future state's Panhandle on a fruitless search for gold. The armored soldiers must have been a bizarre sight to the people they encountered—probably the Wichita tribal farmers and hunters whose villages dotted the area. Most of the residents of this land were members of the Caddo confederation and lived in what would become the southeastern corner of the state. Osage and Quapaw Indians lived farther north, while Lipan and Kiowa Apache communities followed the bison herds in the west. Comanches and Kiowas also arrived in the years before the United States was formed.

There were others, too, who came to this area. Missionaries and explorers from Spanish Mexico arrived, and later, French fur traders wandered down from Canada. What they brought changed the ways of life for the American-Indian tribes that lived there. The Europeans' horses and guns transformed how the Indian people hunted, traveled, and made war. The newcomers also unknowingly brought deadly diseases such as smallpox and tuberculosis, diseases that the Europeans had grown immune to but were fatal to thousands of American Indians.

The trading of fur and other goods was important in the development of the region that became Oklahoma.

INDIAN TERRITORY

In the late eighteenth century the American Revolution cast a new power into the mix. The United States, spreading out from the Atlantic coast, looked west for opportunities to expand its territory. The United States got its chance in 1803 when France sold the Louisiana Territory—the vast western lands whose rivers drained into the Mississippi River—to the young country.

What later would become Oklahoma was part of that territory. Almost immediately the Americans made their presence felt in that area. Zebulon Pike led a U.S. expedition into the area in 1806. He was followed by trappers, traders, and adventurers keen to discover what surprises the new expanded territories had to offer. The U.S. Army arrived in the 1820s, building Forts Gibson (located in present-day Muscogee County) and Towson (in present-day Choctaw County) to protect U.S. claims from Mexico, which owned neighboring Texas at the time. During the next four decades the army would build a half dozen more forts in the area.

But it would be a while before white settlers followed. In the 1830s the United States decided that the area would become a territory for American Indians who had been forced off their ancestral lands back east. Tribes expelled from the eastern states would be forced to accept land in this Indian Territory. Until this arrangement was broken at the end of the century by the U.S. government, Indian Territory was a place uniquely separate from the rest of the United States.

The relocation of these tribes to Indian Territory is one of the most distressing chapters of American history. Whole communities were forced to walk cross-country at gunpoint, and by water from the Mississippi to the Arkansas River, abandoning their land and possessions and enduring enormous hardships along the way. One-third of the Cherokee Nation died on the Trail of Tears, as they called the route from their eastern homes to Indian Territory. The Choctaw, Creek, Seminole, and Chickasaw tribes followed similar hard trails to an uncertain future.

Working with very little, though, these "Five Civilized Tribes" adapted remarkably well to their strange new home. The Cherokees and Choctaws became prosperous cotton growers. Creeks became hog and cattle farmers, as did the Chickasaws, who also herded goats and sheep. The tribes had sawmills and cotton gins, and they traded with nearby settlers and even with their old enemy, the U.S. government.

The relocated American Indians set up camp and settled remarkably well in their new environments.

THE CIVIL WAR AND RECONSTRUCTION

In 1861 many Southern states rebelled against the Union over the issue of slavery and formed the Confederate States of America. The bloody war between the states was also fought in the territories. For four years the Indian Territory was a battle zone. Several of the newly arrived tribes had long owned African slaves. Partly for this reason, many American Indians decided to support the slaveholding Confederacy when the Civil War began. Both the Union and the Confederacy sought the support of the tribes and coveted their food, their horses, and the lead they mined for bullets. Ten thousand people—a fifth of the population of Indian Territory—died during the Civil War or of the diseases and starvation that followed it.

Indian Territory never really recovered from the war. At its beginning, tribes such as the Cherokees were "the wealthiest people in the West," wrote observer J. H. Beadle. "In 1865 their country was almost a waste; the people in extreme poverty. But they came back from the war and sadly went to work again." To punish tribes for their support of the rebels, the U.S. government took away much of their land and assigned it to tribes it was driving out of other parts of the country. Pawnees, Peorias, Ottawas, Wyandots, and Miamis took up residence as farmers in the Indian Territory. Other tribes, however, such as the Cheyenne, Kiowa, Comanche, and Arapaho, who were more hunters than farmers and were used to ranging openly across large hunting grounds, had difficulty adjusting to life confined on small reservations. By the end of this second wave of relocations, more than twenty tribes had reservations in Indian Territory.

American citizens were still barred from settling in Indian Territory, but this did not stop the settlers from coming anyway. Their presence grew greater with every passing year.

As the period called Reconstruction dawned after the Civil War, the U.S. government demanded that the Five Civilized Tribes of Oklahoma abolish slavery. Because the Indian population had aligned themselves with the Southern Confederacy, which lost the war, the U.S. authorities also required that the American Indians sign agreements allowing railroads to be built across the territory. Not surprisingly, the tribes also were forced to surrender much of their land. Toward this end, much of the western portion of what would become Oklahoma was taken from the American-Indian population. Ranchers from Texas began driving cattle across the territory to the railheads in Kansas. Others arrived to mine coal to fuel the trains. As a result, Indian Territory became home to a growing number of white newcomers during the 1870s and 1880s.

Soon the railroads were laying tracks across Indian Territory. Those powerful companies wanted a string of non-Indian towns along the rails to make their railroad businesses more profitable. White hopefuls clamored to be allowed to settle in Indian Territory. "Our people believe," declared Representative James N. Burnes to Congress, "that if it is lawful for a man with a vast herd of cattle to go into that territory, it is lawful for the settler to go there with his wife and little ones." Congress also listened to government officials in charge of Indian affairs who hoped that by allowing open settlement, American Indian traditions would be lost and thus the Indian people would be forced to adapt to an American lifestyle. By the late 1880s a movement was actually under way to take Indian Territory away from the Indians.

Ranchers from Texas drove cattle through Oklahoma on a dirt route known as the Chisholm Trail.

THE OLD CHISHOLM TRAIL

"The Old Chisholm Trail" was the hit song of the 1870s. It starts out with the age-old ballad singer's invitation to "listen to my tale" and proceeds through literally hundreds of two-line verses to tell the tale of every adventure and misadventure that befell cowboys and their cattle as they made their way north on the trail from Texas through Oklahoma to the slaughterhouses and railroad depot in Abilene, Kansas.

I started up the trail October twenty-third,
I started up the trail with the U-2 heard. *Chorus*

On a ten-dollar horse and a forty-dollar saddle,
I'm a-goin' to punch in Texas cattle. *Chorus*

I jumped in the saddle an' I grabbed a-holt the horn,
Best durn cowboy ever was born. *Chorus*

I'm up in the morning before daylight,
And before I sleep the moon shines bright. *Chorus*

It's bacon and beans 'most every day,
I'd just as soon be eating prairie hay. *Chorus*

Cloudy in the west and she looks like rain,
And my damned old slicker's in the wagon again. *Chorus*

The wind began to blow and the rain began to fall,
It looked, by grab, like we was gonna lose 'em all. *Chorus*

I went to the boss to draw my roll,
He had me figured out nine dollars in the hole. *Chorus*

So me and the boss we had a little chat,
And I hit him in the face wuth my old slouch hat. *Chorus*

So the boss said to me, "Well, I'll fire you—
Not only you but the whole damn crew." *Chorus*

Well, I'm going back home to draw my money,
Going back home to see my honey. *Chorus*

With my knees in the saddle and my feet to the sky,
I'll quit punching cattle in the Sweet Bye and Bye. *Chorus*

LAND RUSH

In 1887 the grass still grew and the water still flowed, but that year the U.S. government broke the "permanent" agreements it had made a half-century earlier. It decided to carve tribal lands in Indian Territory into 160-acre (65-ha) allotments and distribute them to individual American-Indian owners. The remaining land in Indian Territory would be opened to new settlers.

There was no stopping this plan once it started. Some of the newly designated "surplus" land was awarded to white homesteaders by lottery. The rest was offered to whoever claimed it in a series of famous land rushes. The first of these land rushes began on April 22, 1889. Guns fired at noon, and 50,000 settlers raced from the eastern border to stake their claims. Some arrived at likely spots to find camps that were obviously more than a few hours old—they'd been beaten by settlers who'd jumped the gun. A few of these Sooners (so named because they rushed the land sooner than they were supposed to) were ejected. Nevertheless, plenty of others were not. Despised at first for their dishonesty, the Sooners were later celebrated in Oklahoma folklore for their frontier cunning.

In 1889 homesteaders staked claims in the Oklahoma land rush.

By the end of the frantic day, every inch of land at the center of present-day Oklahoma had been snapped up. Oklahoma City and other towns witnessed their early beginnings in a matter of hours. Cowboy Evan Barnard, who had worked in Indian Territory before the land rush, was there. The night after the great rush, he recalled, "lights flickered all over the country from the campfires of the settlers. It was a great change for the cowpunchers to see the great cattle country transferred in a day from a region with thousands of cattle to one with thousands of people moving about. We wondered what they would do to make a living."

THE LAND RUSH OF 1889

Arthur Dunham, a teenaged railroad worker, watched the first Oklahoma land rush. He wrote:

I stood on a box car along side the depot at the zero hour of 12 o'clock noon. My astonishment was complete—people seemed to spring up as if by magic as far as the eye could reach. I could see them racing in every direction, some on horses, some in vehicles, and a greater number on foot. They were carrying all sorts of impedimenta—some had spades, some stakes, some clothing, some had handbags, some had pots and pans, or other cooking utensils. My words are not adequate to describe the scene. I then commenced to realize that history was in the making.

Cowboy Bernard was right to wonder. Many of these settlers, and those who joined the land rushes that followed, were ill prepared to make a farm succeed. For every successful farm there were abandoned claims; for every growing town there was a ghost town or an exhausted community struggling against harsh conditions it hadn't foreseen. The rush for land was matched by a quiet retreat of broken dreams.

The land that defeated settlers abandoned often wound up in the hands of big landlords. As new waves of poor farmers arrived to pursue dreams of a prairie farm, they found little land to own, but plenty to rent.

POPULATION GROWTH: 1900–2000

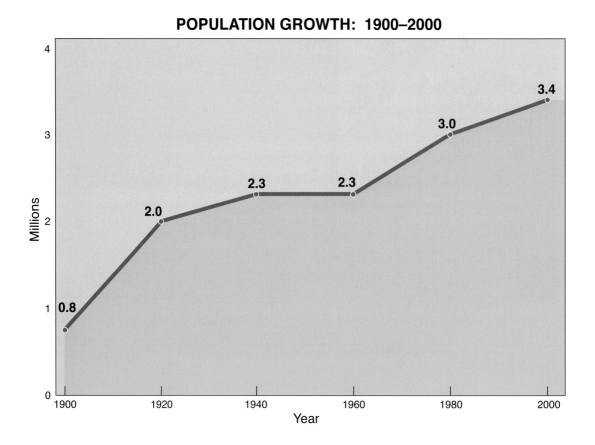

By the early twentieth century tenant farming, or sharecropping, was bigger in Oklahoma than in any other state. Landlords would let sharecroppers work the land in exchange for a portion of the crops they grew. Sharecroppers never got rich on the deal. Most years, they counted themselves lucky just to survive.

STATEHOOD AND OIL

In 1905 a convention for the Indian State of Sequoyah was held, a constitution was written, and an election was held. More than 165,000 voters favored recognition of this Indian state, but officials in Washington ignored the movement altogether.

By 1906 all the land that had once been held in common by the several tribes of Indian Territory had been divided among individuals—tribal members and non-Indian newcomers. So many new settlers had come to the area during this time that only one in ten residents were American Indian.

The Oklahoma state delegates voted to elect William "Alfalfa Bill" Murray of Tishomingo to be the president of the state's constitutional convention. A constitution was completed the following year and on September 17, 1907, all parties ratified it. On November 16, 1907, President Theodore Roosevelt declared Oklahoma to be the forty-sixth state of the Union.

After statehood, a lot of newcomers were attracted to Oklahoma, not just because of the offer of land but because Oklahoma was experiencing an economic boom caused by the discovery of petroleum. The newest American state sat atop fantastic amounts of oil and gas. New inventions such as the automobile boosted demand for oil, and new technologies made collecting and selling it highly profitable.

The change in the air was apparent to such visitors as German sociologist Max Weber, who wrote in 1905, "There is a fabulous bustle here, and I cannot help but find tremendous fascination in it, despite the stench of petroleum and the fumes." Oil put Oklahoma on the economic map. Folksinger Woody Guthrie expressed it this way: "Oil was more than gold ever was or will be, because you can't make any hair salve or perfume, TNT, or roofing material or drive a car with just gold. You can't pipe that gold back East and run them big factories, either."

Oklahoma City grew around its own oil fields during the boom years. CITY WELL HURLS "LIQUID GOLD" HIGH OVER OIL DERRICK, reported a 1928 headline. Soon, hundreds of wells were tapping the city's oil field, which was one of the nation's largest producers during the 1930s. To this day Oklahoma is the only state to have an oil well in front of its state capitol.

Oil was once called black gold, and wells like this one were found all over the state.

OIL'S BLOODY UNDERSIDE

Tulsa grew on the strength of the oil boom. The diversity and promise of urban life, however, also contained the seeds of racial intolerance. One vicious day in 1921, Tulsa fell into chaos. A white lynch mob threatened to kill a black man falsely accused of assaulting a white woman. A group of armed blacks confronted the mob. The conflict exploded into a day of brutal violence in which as many as three hundred African Americans may have died. Gunfire and fire-bombings all but leveled the Greenwood neighborhood where most black Tulsans lived. The riot "may have been the worst incident of racial violence in American history," says writer Scott Ellsworth.

Kinney Booker, eight years old at the time, remembered a narrow escape after white rioters set his family's house ablaze. "At first, I hated all white people," he admitted. He recalled, though, that a white family sheltered his family after the riot.

Young Booker, like most other Tulsans, tried hard to forget the terrible event. Schoolchildren rarely heard it discussed in class. In 1997, though, the Oklahoma state legislature formed the Tulsa Race Riot Commission to investigate and set the record straight. Oklahoma schoolchildren now use the Tulsa Race Riot of 1921 as an opportunity to think about and discuss racial intolerance.

OKLAHOMA'S BLACK WALL STREET

The combination of the Civil War and the freeing of slaves plus the economic boom caused by the discovery of oil brought many African Americans to Oklahoma in search of work. Job opportunities in the early years of the nineteenth century were running high in the state and thus encouraged the migration. Soon black communities were not only built, they were also very successful. Black businesspeople owned banks, newspapers, barber shops, hotels, and retail stores. The African-American community called Greenwood, which was located near Tulsa, flourished. Some 11,000 residents lived in Greenwood. Some were doctors and lawyers. Others were owners of restaurants—there were over two hundred in the area. Through the economic success of Greenwood, black millionaires were made—a stunning achievement in its time. The community was so successful that Greenwood took on the nickname of Black Wall Street, a reference to the economic center in New York City.

But something very wrong occurred on the night of May 21, 1921. Tensions between whites and blacks around the Tulsa area had been running high, especially after the lynching of two black prisoners in 1919. So when Dick Rowland, a black man, was arrested for allegedly assaulting Sarah Page, a white woman, tempers flared. A mob of some two thousand whites gathered around the jailhouse. Meanwhile, suspecting that the white mob had planned another lynching, a small group of blacks came to the jailhouse to protect the prisoner. In the heat of the confrontation between the two groups, gunshots were fired and several blacks and whites lay dead. What ensued over the next couple of days was one of the most devastating race riots in U.S. history. In the process Greenwood was destroyed. After the riots broke out and fires were set, what had once been called Black Wall Street had been burned to the ground.

Black smoke billows from fires during the race riot of 1921 in Greenwood.

No one has an accurate count of deaths. Some estimate that three hundred Greenwood residents were killed in the riots. Others believe it was in the thousands and that the bodies were secretly buried in mass graves. What is known is that thousands of the survivors of this riot were left homeless. In the meantime, Rowland, the man who was accused of assaulting a white woman, was acquitted of all charges.

Greenwood residents struggled to rebuild their community in the years that followed. They were partially successful. During the 1930s and 1940s some businesses were rebuilt and became a haven of black culture. By 1941, six hundred black-owned businesses were thriving. Another blow to the community was coming, though. Prior to World War II, the City of Tulsa, under the influence of segregation laws, had barred African Americans from shopping in South Tulsa. Such ordinances actually profited the African-American businesses in Greenwood. Since blacks had nowhere else to buy food or to seek services, black wealth stayed within the community. But after the war, Tulsa revoked the ban on shopping, which led to an insurmountable decrease in sales in the Greenwood business district. Greenwood, to this day, has not regained its economic edge. Today, only thirteen black-owned businesses remain.

Details of the riot in Tulsa were hushed in the years that followed, until 1997, when pressure for reparations was applied to the Oklahoma government. In 1997 the government complied by establishing the Tulsa Race Riot Commission. The commission was ordered to study the events of the riot and to develop a historical account. The commission's final report was delivered four years later, on February 21, 2001. Some recommendations of the commission included paying the survivors of Greenwood or their descendants for their losses. Another recommendation was that the remains of the victims should be reburied and marked with a memorial to honor them. A few months later, in June 2001, the Oklahoma state legislature passed the 1921 Tulsa Race Riot Reconciliation Act. Although the act did not cover all the commission's recommendations, a college scholarship program for descendants of the victims was provided and a memorial was erected. To this day, however, Greenwood remains an impoverished area, just a shadow of its former self.

DEPRESSION, DROUGHT, AND THE DUST BOWL

The Great Depression affected every American in the 1930s, but it may have hit Oklahomans hardest. Like all other Americans, Oklahomans confronted a wrecked economy, but they also were forced to endure the ravages of the Dust Bowl. Western Oklahoma was at the heart of the area where drought, high winds, and plow-damaged fields combined to create disaster in the 1930s. Windstorms lifted the rich topsoil from the fields and hurled it through the air, burying some farms to the rooftops and leaving others surrounded only by dusty fields that could not grow crops.

One-third of a million Oklahomans, mostly poor sharecroppers from the western plains, abandoned the state during the 1930s to seek a livelihood elsewhere. Many found, after hard traveling, that work

Desperate days of the Dust Bowl caused people to walk away from farms that had been in their families for many generations.

was just as scarce everywhere and decent and humane treatment was even scarcer. Wherever they went, the Dust Bowl migrants were at once pitied and feared. Whether they came from Oklahoma or other hard-hit states such as Texas or Kansas, they were called Okies. The migrants soon learned that the word Okie meant poor, stupid, dirty, and desperate. Over time, though, the shame associated with the word shifted to pride. Like the Sooners before them, the Okies eventually became heroes of Oklahoma folklore.

WAR, PEACE, AND PROSPERITY

As suddenly as the Great Depression and the Dust Bowl had knocked Oklahoma to pieces, World War II, oddly enough, helped put it back together. Even before the United States entered the war in 1941, Oklahoma was building Tinker Air Force Base near Oklahoma City. With the expansion of Vance Air Force Base near Enid and Fort Sill Military Reservation near Lawton, Oklahoma became home to some of the most important military installations in the country. Thousands of soldiers trained at Oklahoma bases during the war. The state distinguished itself in combat as well. Oklahomans in the Forty-Fifth Infantry division, many of them American Indians, fought valiantly in Europe. "Your division is one of the best, if not the best division in the history of American armies," General George Patton told them.

J. O. Smith of Okemah served in the Forty-Fifth division. "Lots of men died. Lots of men were wounded. But we made it, by God. We had initiative, and we knew we had to do some real bold fighting," he recalled. "So we got it all together and got the job done. Just a bunch of hard-core Okies."

During World War II, Oklahoma was home to some of the most important military air bases.

Memories of the Depression, the Dust Bowl, and wartime sacrifice began to fade in the decades following the war. Although agriculture, after the war, became less prominent in the Oklahoma economy, industry began its dramatic rise during the 1950s. The state government encouraged new businesses to move to Oklahoma, and they did. Companies that manufacture space equipment, electronic plants, and even a government agency, the Federal Aviation Administration, moved to Oklahoma. Construction jobs also fueled the economy as the state moved into the 1960s. Several dams were built, which created some of the many man-made lakes. From the dams came hydroelectric power.

In 1970 the McClellan-Kerr Arkansas River Navigation System was completed, connecting Tulsa with the Mississippi River, which then leads to the Gulf of Mexico. Prior to this system, the Arkansas River, as it runs in south Oklahoma, was too shallow to allow heavy barge traffic. But today, through a series of locks, the river system means that Oklahoma has a busy port on the outskirts of Tulsa.

THE OKLAHOMA CITY BOMBING

Early in the morning of April 19, 1995, workers arrived as usual at their offices at the Murrah Federal Building in downtown Oklahoma City, saying good-bye to their children at the doors of the building's day-care center. A few minutes later, as everyone was settling in, Oklahoma was changed forever.

"Everything is the blackest black you can imagine, and I don't hear any noise. But I can feel the force of the air carry me, and I know I'm flying in the air. . . . I can hear the sound of those concrete floors collapsing on each other right around me," lawyer Duane Miller said later. "When the floor noise stops, the only other thing I can hear is the sound of one man calling for help." A bomb had exploded, tearing the building apart. At the time, this was the nation's worst brush with terrorism. The bombing caused the violent deaths of 168 people and another 600 were injured. Some days later Timothy McVeigh and Terry Nichols were arrested for the crime. In 2001 McVeigh was executed. Nichols was sentenced to life in prison.

Today the bomb site has been transformed into a public memorial of great dignity for the victims. The memorial includes a reflecting pool and a field filled with 168 stone chairs, one for each person killed in the bombing. It is a place for visitors to meditate on a senseless tragedy and on the sensitive and generous spirit of the people of Oklahoma who tried to come to their fellow Oklahomans' rescue.

Victims of the Oklahoma City bombing are remembered through this national memorial.

ECONOMIC GROWTH IN THE TWENTY-FIRST CENTURY

Though the U.S. economy was struggling in 2008, Oklahoma was enjoying economic growth. The state had created new jobs at a rate that exceeded the nation's, winning Oklahoma sixth place in the highest employment growth in the United States. The top three biggest businesses in Oklahoma that year were the state government, the retail store Walmart, and Tinker Air Force Base, outside of Oklahoma City. According to Natalie Shirley, the Oklahoma secretary of Commerce and Tourism, Oklahoma is ranked as one of the most business-friendly states in the country. This is because of the low cost of living in the state together with a great quality of life. Also in 2008, while the prices of houses in other states were sharply declining, Oklahoma was ranked number one in home value gains. This was a positive sign for the Oklahoma economy. It was also a signal that there was a demand for houses, which means that people were still seeking out Oklahoma as a place to call home.

Oklahoma has gone through many changes over the years. At one time, when American Indians were forced to live there, it was a place of banishment. At another time, Oklahoma was a place of dreams as settlers rushed the land to stake their claim. Then the crippling years of the Dust Bowl era dried up many people's hopes. But not too much later, oil brought the sparkle back into Oklahomans' eyes as prosperity filled their pockets. As the dusty days of the cowboys began to fade, the days of the oil barons moved into the headlights.

In 2007, as Oklahomans celebrated the state's centennial with parades, festivities, music, and exhibitions, many told stories about the past, while others looked ahead to the future. The state has gone

In 2008 Oklahoma's business center was thriving, while much of the U.S. economy was struggling.

through many changes in the past century, but the land has remained pretty much the same. The people of Oklahoma may be moving from the more rural lands to the cities, but their frontier spirit and their abiding pride in their state is still very evident.

Chapter Three

A Mix of Cultures

For a long time, Oklahoma was an agricultural state, with many people living out their lives on farms and ranches. But the state's modern population has been steadily moving away from the rural sections and settling around Oklahoma's cities. In the past the population of the area that now encompasses Oklahoma was completely American Indian. Today the Indian population in Oklahoma continues to be significant, though the white population is dominant. Despite the fact that most Oklahomans are white, the cultural mix is diverse and growing. Besides having one of the largest populations of American Indians and a prominent number of African Americans, Latinos in Oklahoma are a fast-growing group, and an increasing number of people with Asian backgrounds have made Oklahoma their home. The estimated 2007 U.S. Census for the entire population for Oklahoma was 3,617,316, with a projection of there being almost four million residents in the state by the year 2030.

REGIONAL CROSSROADS

There are other, more subtle, regional variances in the lives and histories of the people of Oklahoma. For example, the cultural backgrounds of

Even though Oklahoma is a state with a diverse cultural mix of people, today the American-Indian population continues to be significant.

the people who settled in northern Oklahoma came from Midwestern states such as Kansas. Southern Oklahoma, by contrast, was peopled by migrants from such southern states as Texas and Arkansas. These varied settlers brought their own cultural styles that persist today. Grain elevators tower over northern towns such as Alva and Perry. The northern section of Oklahoma is populated by farmers, for the most part, who came with Midwestern sensibilities. In the southern portion, cotton wagons rumble through such small towns as Durant and Hugo. There the smell of southern barbecue reigns, reflecting more of a traditionally southern culture.

Even though each section of the state is affected by the residents' cultural differences, Oklahomans are brought together by their western sensibilities. In general, most relate to the lives of cowboys. It is true that only a few Oklahomans really have much to do with horses, cattle, and ranches today, but the western influence is apparent. Oklahoma City, for instance, is home to the National Cowboy & Western Heritage Museum, and many of the state's museums specialize in cowboy and American-Indian art. Throw in the numerous rodeos and American-Indian powwows and the western atmosphere is complete.

Oklahoma is a state recognized for its western flair.

RURAL OKLAHOMA

Though most Oklahomans live in cities, rural life is what residents and outsiders alike usually think of when they picture the state. Oklahoma doesn't call to mind city skylines as much as soft green crops of winter wheat broken by patches of bright red dirt. Many of the farmers are descendants of the first white settlers who came from places in Europe such as Germany, Ireland, and England.

Even those who do not live on farms treasure connections to their agricultural backgrounds by sending their children to the classic rural club, the Future Farmers of America (FFA). There the younger generations learn the skills and rewards of an agricultural career and travel to events that the club sponsors. "We've seen a whole lot more country than other kids in our school," Jamie Hix boasted. Some of the organization's meetings draw in whole communities. "Everybody in town baked pies," recounted Melissa Davis, from Oaks. "There were four hundred to five hundred pies," she said, at the state FFA convention she attended.

NATIVE AMERICA

There are license plates in the state that boast that Oklahoma is really "Native America." There is a reason behind this nickname. In 2007 it was estimated that almost 300,000 American Indians live in Oklahoma, more than in any state besides California. Eight percent of Oklahomans are American Indian, a higher percentage than any state except Alaska and New Mexico. Depending on who's counting, up to sixty-seven different tribes are represented—by far the largest number of different Indian cultures in the United States.

Oklahoma's Indian people struggle to preserve cultural traditions. A Creek or Muscogee day-care and cultural center in Okmulgee brings in storytellers and artists and serves kids Creek foods such as fry bread and wild grape dumplings. The center takes pains to teach young children Creek, which—like many American-Indian languages—is in danger of dying out. The focus on children is important, according to Creek chief A. D. Ellis, "You don't wait until they're twenty or thirty" to build an interest in native culture. Alexis Crosley, the father of a child who attends the center, agreed. "I don't know how to speak Creek," he admitted. "I want my kids to know all of that."

Perhaps the best example of American Indians working together to preserve their heritage is found at a powwow. Summer is powwow season in Oklahoma, with events scheduled for every weekend all over the state.

To preserve cultural traditions, a father tells his children stories about their ancestors.

ETHNIC OKLAHOMA

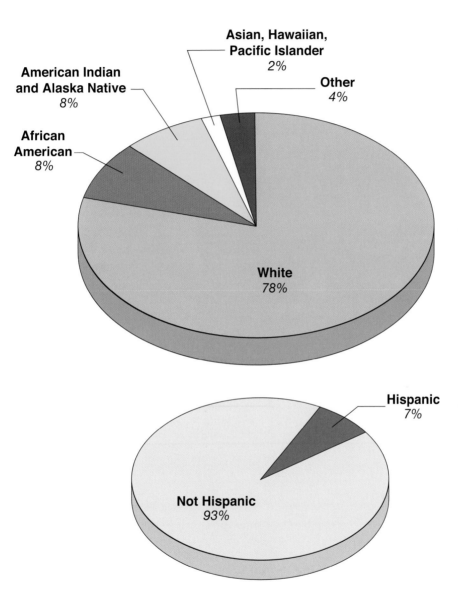

Asian, Hawaiian,
Pacific Islander
2%

Other
4%

American Indian
and Alaska Native
8%

African
American
8%

White
78%

Hispanic
7%

Not Hispanic
93%

*Note: A person of Cuban, Mexican, Puerto Rican, South or Central American,
or other Spanish culture or origin, regardless of race, is defined as Hispanic.*

THE FORTUNATE HUNTER

Folktales aren't always serious. Many Indian legends are intended to make people laugh. This tall tale was told by an elderly Cherokee storyteller, Gahnô, many years ago.

A hunter had been sick for a long time. Finally he felt well, but also very hungry. He went into the woods to hunt.

The hunter spied a deer standing across a stream. He took aim and shot. His arrow pierced the deer's neck and pinned its quivering body to the trunk of a tree.

The hunter squatted to remove his boots so he could cross the stream. He felt something wriggling underneath him, and found that he was sitting on a rabbit. The rabbit was dying, so he grabbed it and struck it against the ground to finish it off. The rabbit whacked a sleeping family of quails and killed them all, too.

The hunter crossed the stream, his boots trailing in the water. When he tried to put them on, he found that they were brimming with glistening, flopping fish.

The hunter yanked the arrow to free the deer's body. From the arrow hole gushed honey—a beehive was hidden in a hollow of the tree.

The hunter collected the deer, rabbit, quails, fish, and honey, and hauled them home. He was still hungry, but life was going to be good now!

Powwows combine dance, song, camaraderie, food, and the celebration of tradition. Each powwow is unique, but all have common features and a common origin. Not long ago the famous Osage ballerina Maria Tallchief remembered that American Indians "were subject to government edicts which were designed to destroy tribal customs." American Indians quietly preserved their old ceremonies and embraced what would become new traditions. "We didn't know it then," said Jerry Bread, "but these social gatherings were to evolve into what today is called a powwow." Oklahoma, with its complex mix of Indian cultures, has led the country in developing the modern powwow. The "World's Biggest Powwow" is part of Oklahoma City's Red Earth Festival, which draws participants from more than one hundred tribes, traveling to Oklahoma from all the other states.

Song is one basic element of the powwow. "From ancient times the people have sung in times of trouble and danger, to cure the sick, to confound their enemies," explained Jimalee Burton, a Cherokee. Powwows help to preserve those traditions, as a Kiowa song by Leonard Cozad demonstrates:

Where are the old people?
The *Kiowa* people?
The *songs* are the only things we have left, *now*.
All the old people went somewhere,
They're *gone*.
And all we've got left now are these songs,
To *sing*.

Also basic to every powwow is dancing. A typical powwow features several long dances spread out over a couple of days. "Powwow dancers are athletes," said Darrell Wildcat, a member of the Euchee and Kiowa tribes. "Many dances, especially the women's Fancy Shawl and the Fancy War Dance, require tremendous strength and stamina."

BLACK TOWNS ON THE PRAIRIE

Oklahoma's varied culture also features mostly black towns founded by former slaves after the Civil War. Unlike freed slaves elsewhere, many living in Indian Territory gained allotments of land when

American Indians celebrate their traditional customs during powwows.

the American-Indian tribal lands were divided up. That award allowed them to found almost thirty black towns, more than were established in all the other states combined. Residents of these towns enjoyed real power in their communities at a time when most African Americans were excluded from politics and other aspects of economic and public life.

Only thirteen of these towns remain today, and many of them are shrinking. "The Great Depression . . . was devastating to the all-black towns," said historian Curry Ballard. Many black residents left to find economic opportunities elsewhere, and few returned. Boley is one of those surviving all-black towns that looks as if it might endure. This town of fewer than 1,000 residents swells to 15,000 every Memorial Day weekend when it hosts the Boley rodeo, an event that also features barbecue, music, and a parade.

RECENT IMMIGRANTS

Though groups of Asian Americans and Latinos make up the smaller segments of Oklahoma's population, their numbers are climbing.

The Asian-American population made an impact on the state in 1975 after refugees from the Vietnam War came to Oklahoma City. In the more than thirty years since, the Asian-American population has grown, creating the Asia District north of town, a business and residential section of the city. In the Asia District people can find authentic Asian foods, nightclubs, grocery stores, and shops. Besides the Vietnamese, other Asian cultures represented in Oklahoma include Japanese, Filipino, Chinese, Indian, and Korean Americans.

The Latino culture is the most populous among the newer immigrants, with figures estimated to be around 179,300 in 2007. This is the fastest growing minority group in Oklahoma. Many Hispanic Americans come from Mexico in search of jobs. Some arrive without proper paperwork from the U.S. federal government. In recent years illegal immigration has become a topic of heated discussions in Oklahoma and across the nation. In 2007 the state government passed one of the strictest laws in all the states concerning illegal immigrants. The result is that many Latinos are leaving the state to live elsewhere.

POPULATION
DENSITY

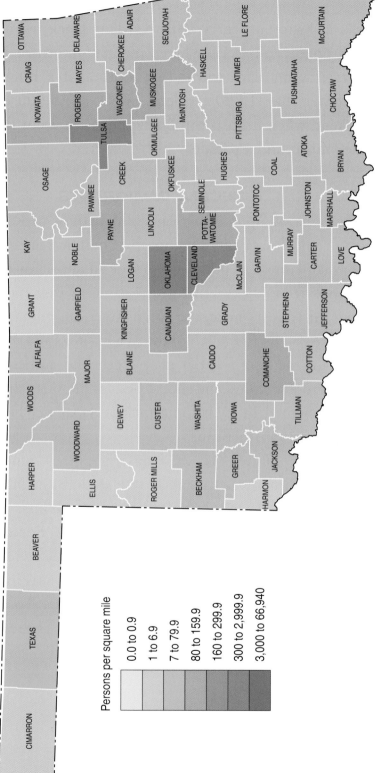

Persons per square mile

0.0 to 0.9
1 to 6.9
7 to 79.9
80 to 159.9
160 to 299.9
300 to 2,999.9
3,000 to 66,940

CELEBRATING TOGETHER

People from east and west, north and south, and all places in between in the state, gather together each year at the Oklahoma State Fair, held every fall in Tulsa. The fair is a big party featuring events and exhibits from every corner of the state. Some of the exhibits are traditional, such as livestock judging and midway rides. Others aren't—such as Sharon Bu Mann's sculpture of a cow and two children, which was displayed in a big glass refrigerator. It would have melted otherwise, for it was made of half a ton of butter. "I always told my children never to play with their food," Bu Mann admitted. Fairgoers enjoy odd treats that reappear every year, such as pork chop sandwiches and fried pickles.

Almost every town seems to hold some kind of festival, and many of them have food themes. You could eat your way across Oklahoma, celebrating chili in Tulsa, strawberries in Stilwell, huckleberries in Jay, watermelons in Rush Springs, and cheese in Watonga. El Reno celebrates Fried Onion Burger Day, and Vinita offers the World's Largest Calf Fry Festival and Cook-Off. For dessert, there's Okmulgee's Pecan Festival, Wewoka's Sorghum Day, and Erick's Honey Festival.

Celebrations happen in many different cities across the state. An example is Juneteenth, the holiday marking the end of slavery after the Civil War. Towns from Tulsa to Enid to Ponca City observe it with parades, picnics, music, and games. Some celebrations are small affairs, often organized by a single church congregation. Others, such as Oklahoma City's, attract lots of participants. "This is not a black thing, not a white thing, but something all of Oklahoma City can be proud of," said Jeffrey Carolina, who helps organize the celebration.

PANHANDLE COLESLAW

There's a lot of awful coleslaw in this world—droopy, soggy, chewed up, or sweet as candy. But in Oklahoma they know how to make coleslaw right, and they'll serve it with almost any meal. It's incredibly easy to make—you won't even need the recipe after your second or third batch. Be sure to have an adult help you with the chopping.

    1 small green cabbage
    2 carrots, peeled
    2 tablespoons vinegar
    1 teaspoon sugar
    1 teaspoon mustard
    1/2 teaspoon caraway seeds (optional)
    salt and pepper to taste

Peel the tough outer leaves off the cabbage and cut it in half. Cut out the center core. Working slowly and carefully with a sharp knife, shave off thin, lacy slices into a big bowl. Grate the carrots into the same bowl.

In another bowl, combine the other ingredients to make the dressing. Mix thoroughly and pour it over the cabbage and carrots. Toss well, then refrigerate for a little while before serving.

Everyone makes coleslaw a bit differently. Experiment until you have your own perfect recipe. Some "secret ingredients" to try: chopped peanuts, grated onions, crushed garlic, fresh lemon juice—or anything else that seems right to you.

Oklahoma's rich history continues to be remembered and celebrated, as seen by this monument depicting the state's early settlers.

Traveling throughout the state, especially in the bigger cities of Oklahoma City and Tulsa, is like a trip through history. Influences of the past, as seen through the many different cultures, are alive and well in Oklahoma. Memories of Indian Territory as well as the land rushes and the freed slaves who set up homes here have left their traces. But the past is not the only thing that has influenced the lives of Oklahoma's people. With the growing impact of immigrants from all over the world, Oklahoma's modern population reflects the future—the bridging and coming together of all the cultures of the world.

Chapter Four

How Things Are Done

"No other place in the world offers a more gruesome study of democracy in the raw—nor of how thoroughly it can be cooked," Oklahoman George Milburn wrote a half century ago about his state. True, Oklahoma's early politics were often chaotic and colorful, but today the state has a government that suits the majority's desire for conservatism and low taxes, one that stays out of most aspects of daily life, reflecting the independent nature of Oklahomans.

As an example of this independent nature, Governor Brad Henry, in his 2003 inaugural address, stressed the limited role that government should play in solving Oklahoman's challenges of the future: "Government serves basic and necessary functions, but it doesn't hold all the answers. This administration will look to the private sector and public-private partnerships to get the job done when government can't do it alone. We have much to learn from private ventures and charitable institutions. We can use joint ventures and partnerships to accomplish new goals."

The Oklahoma State Capitol, located in Oklahoma City, remains today as the only state capitol grounds in the United States with active oil rigs.

INSIDE GOVERNMENT

Some of the biggest decisions affecting U.S. states are made by the federal government in Washington, D.C. But other important laws touching everyday life are made, enforced, and interpreted by state governments.

As with the national constitution, the constitution of Oklahoma divides the work among three branches of government: executive, legislative, and judicial.

Executive

The governor, the chief executive, is chosen in a statewide election every four years. Other elected executive officials include the lieutenant governor and the attorney general.

The governor oversees the operation of the departments and agencies that make up the rest of the executive branch. These include the department of corrections, which operates the jails and prisons; the Department of Education, which oversees the schools; and the Department of Public Safety, which issues driver's licenses and manages the Oklahoma Highway Patrol. These departments and others are designed to carry out laws passed by the legislature—making sure that prison and school cafeterias don't serve spoiled food, for example, and catching drivers who break traffic laws. The governor also works with the legislature to decide which political issues will be considered every year, and either signs their proposals into law or rejects—vetoes—them. The legislature has the final say, however, for it can override a governor's veto with the approval of two-thirds of the members of each house.

Legislative

The legislature (the 48-member senate and the 101-member house of representatives) is the lawmaking branch of state government. The legislature meets every year to debate proposals for new laws. If both houses vote for a proposal it is sent to the governor, whose approval makes it law. Representatives are elected to two-year terms and senators to four-year terms.

Oklahoma's twenty-sixth governor, Brad Henry, was first elected to office in 2002.

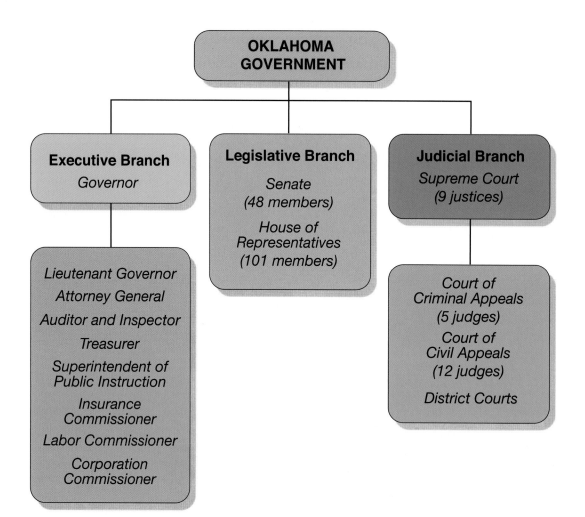

OKLAHOMA GOVERNMENT

Executive Branch
Governor

Lieutenant Governor

Attorney General

Auditor and Inspector

Treasurer

Superintendent of Public Instruction

Insurance Commissioner

Labor Commissioner

Corporation Commissioner

Legislative Branch

Senate
(48 members)

House of Representatives
(101 members)

Judicial Branch
Supreme Court
(9 justices)

Court of Criminal Appeals
(5 judges)

Court of Civil Appeals
(12 judges)

District Courts

Judicial

The judicial branch is the part of Oklahoma government that interprets state law. Judges help decide whether those accused of breaking the law are guilty or innocent. They also consider whether the legislature's decisions and the actions of the executive branch agree with the laws and constitution of Oklahoma.

The backbone of Oklahoma's judicial branch is its system of district courts, which hear cases in twenty-six districts around the state. Above these are the courts of criminal and civil appeals, where disputed rulings from the district courts are reviewed. If there are further disagreements in a civil case, the supreme court can review it, but unlike in most states, Oklahoma's supreme court does not review criminal cases. The court, which has nine justices appointed by the governor and approved by the legislature, does, however, have some management responsibilities over the court of criminal appeals.

TRIBAL GOVERNMENT

The cities and counties of every state have governments, too. But nowhere else are there as many tribal governments as in Oklahoma. Thirty-eight American-Indian tribes have headquarters there—far more than in any other state.

Indians are full citizens both of the United States and of Oklahoma, and many have been leaders in government. (In fact, five of the eleven American Indians who have served in the U.S. Congress represented Oklahoma.) American Indians who are enrolled members of a tribe have rights and responsibilities under the tribe's government, too.

Although each tribe does things a little differently, most have adopted a three-branch government similar to Oklahoma's. A typical tribe elects a chief as executive and a tribal council as legislature, and maintains a tribal court system. A tribe's court system, not Oklahoma's, has jurisdiction over certain crimes and disputes, especially when they occur on Indian land or when a grievance is between tribal members.

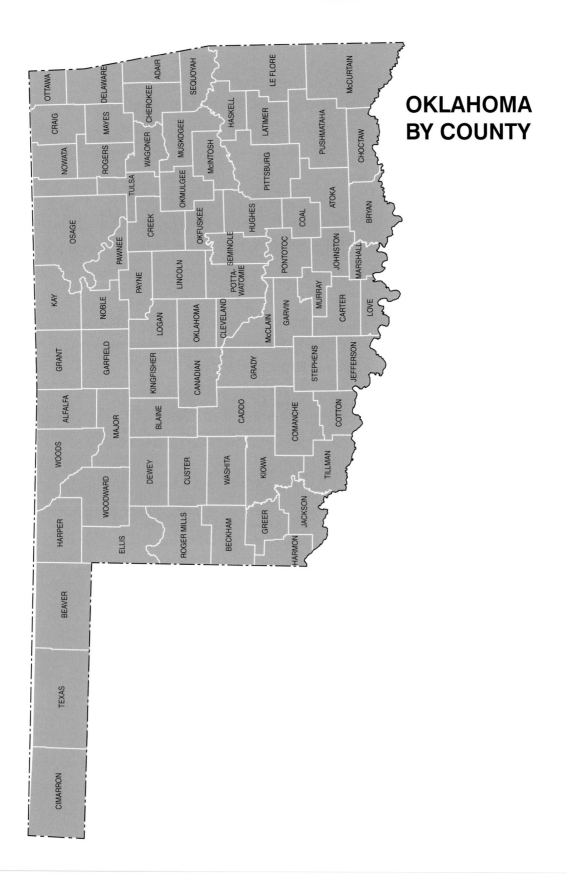

**OKLAHOMA
BY COUNTY**

TOUGH ON CRIME

Oklahoma is tough on crime. About 1 out of every 160 Oklahomans is confined to a jail or prison. Only Texas and Louisiana have higher rates of imprisonment. Part of the reason for this is that longer jail sentences are attached to laws broken than in many other states.

The state also condemns more criminals to death than many other states, and most of its residents strongly support the death penalty. Some believe that children thus learn that crime doesn't pay. Judge Richard Clarke used to conduct trials in schools to give students a taste of how lawbreakers are punished. "I would never want to experience what these people had to," said high school student Brandon Harris after watching the judge in his school lunchroom court sentence three drunk drivers to jail. "I would never do it."

Oklahoma City's tough-on-crime public safety policies contribute to the many inmates that are confined to a prison or jail.

PROMOTING HEALTH IN SCHOOLS

The state congress as well as the governor's wife, Kim Henry, worked on a bill and a program of getting Oklahoma's students in shape in 2008. The legislature focused on passing a bill that calls for more physical activity, while Mrs. Henry focused on a creative way to get teens involved in promoting health.

Beginning with the 2008–09 school year, according to senate bill 1186, authored by State Senator Mary Easley, a Democrat from Tulsa, all Oklahoma public elementary schools have to provide students with an average extra sixty minutes of physical activity each week. This is in addition to the hour of physical education already mandated by state law.

"Over the last few years, schools across Oklahoma and the nation have seen a decrease in physical activity within the school day," Senator Easley said. "As a result, more of our children are obese, creating a potential health crisis in the future. We have a great responsibility to try and reverse this course. This bill is a good beginning to a healthier Oklahoma."

Some of the reasons for this new law were based on startling statistics about the health of the younger generation in Oklahoma. These show that Oklahoma ranks sixth highest among U.S. states for teen obesity; that the state ranks last in the nation for the percent of persons who consume the daily recommended amount of fruits and vegetables; and that obesity is expensive, costing Oklahoma an estimated $1.3 billion annually in health care and other consequences.

The state's First Lady, Kim Henry, also concerned about the health of Oklahoma's children, suggested a different path to educating teenagers about adopting healthier lifestyles. She helped to launch a contest called MyTakeOnHealth: Oklahoma Video Challenge.

Oklahoma encourages students to adopt a healthy lifestyle through regular exercise.

"Young people nationwide face a host of obstacles to good health," Mrs. Henry said. "It's vital that young people get the message, and promote the message, that a healthy life means a happy and productive life." Through the challenge, which ran from October through December in 2008, teens were encouraged to create their own videos that demonstrated the importance of healthy living. The student videos spotlighted topics dealing with good body weight, nutrition, the importance of exercise, and the lethal effects of tobacco and alcohol. Prizes were awarded both to the students who made the winning videos and to their schools.

Chapter Five

From Oil and Cattle to a Modern Economy

Oklahoma's economy has been dominated by farming and oil production from its beginnings as a state. Although both agriculture and petroleum remain important aspects of the state's economy, neither one is as predominant as it used to be. In 2008 the service industry ranked number one. This industry provides services to the residents of the state and includes such employers as the government and the retail sector. Oklahoma's biggest employers today are the state government, which runs schools and other state services; the military, which operates the armed forces bases in the state; and the retail giant Walmart, which sells things like food and clothing.

Typical of the changes that the state is going through is Tulsa's Williams Corporation. This alert company installed fiber-optic cables along its natural gas pipelines, adding telecommunications to an existing energy network. Companies like Williams are adjusting to the new economic environment, supplementing old industries with dramatic new features.

The military is one of Oklahoma's largest employers today.

DOWN ON THE FARM

Though agriculture is not as large a part of Oklahoma's economy as it once was, farmers still occupy an important sector. Statistics for 2007 showed that the state had 82,500 farms. Or, seen in another way, 33.7 million acres (14 million ha) of land in Oklahoma were dedicated to farming. "If they [the farmers] don't make money, we don't make money," explained Cheryl McKelvy, a waitress at Rhonda's Café in Snyder. Consumers as well as businesses that sell food depend on farmers to be successful.

2007 GROSS STATE PRODUCT: $139 Million

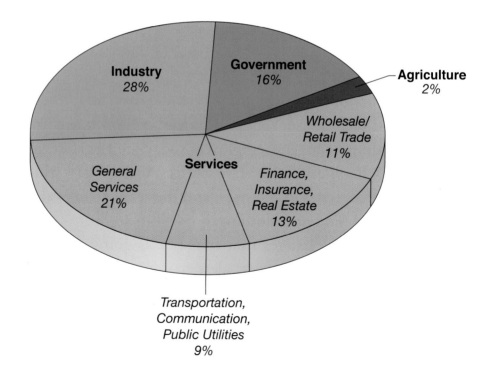

Industry
28%

Government
16%

Agriculture
2%

Wholesale/
Retail Trade
11%

General
Services
21%

Services

Finance,
Insurance,
Real Estate
13%

Transportation,
Communication,
Public Utilities
9%

Oklahoma continues to produce most of the nation's supply of wheat, even though the amount grown in 2008 decreased from the previous year.

Even in good years, farming is tough work. "Everything you see out there's made out of sweat," farmer Ned DeWitt once wrote. "I know to the penny what I had to pay for them pigs and horses and chickens . . . and I know what they'll bring on the market right now, because I've had to put out too much hard work not to know."

Most Oklahoma cropland is planted in wheat, the state's largest agricultural product. Though the amount of wheat grown in Oklahoma in 2008 decreased from the previous year, the state continues to produce most of the nation's supply. Because of the rich soil and the weather, wheat grows best on the old prairie land, on the plains in the central part of the state. Corn, sorghum, and soybeans make up another large portion of agricultural products grown in the state. Cotton is also produced on Oklahoma's farms, but cotton prefers the weather conditions of the southwestern portion of the state. The temperatures are warmer there, though the land is dry and must be irrigated. Other valuable crops grown in the state include strawberries, spinach, beans, and corn, as well as melons and peaches.

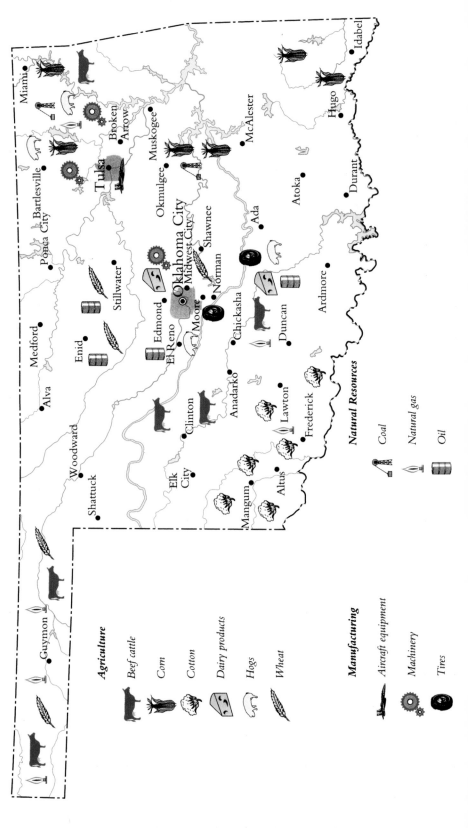

On the rest of the farm and ranch land, cattle, hogs, chickens, and hay (fodder for the animals) are raised. The number of cattle has been increasing in the past decade. In 2008, 5,400,000 cattle for beef were raised in the state. Cattle for beef are shipped all over the nation, while dairy cows, which numbered 69,000 in 2008, are raised close to the state's metropolitan areas, around Tulsa and Oklahoma City especially. This provides dairy farmers easy access to local markets for the milk products.

The number of cattle raised for beef has increased dramatically over the last ten years.

SWINE FACTORIES

In 2008 the U.S. Department of Agriculture estimated the number of hogs in Oklahoma to be around 2.33 million. This made Oklahoma the eighth largest hog-producing state in the nation. Hog production in Oklahoma has increased in the past couple of decades because gigantic "factory" hog farms have opened in the state. In 1992 for example, Seaboard Farms started an enormous hog enterprise in the Panhandle. The company has its own meatpacking plant where hogs are slaughtered and processed into pork chops and bacon.

Some boast that swine factories such as these help the state's rural economy. Over 2,400 people work at the Seaboard plant, for example, but most workers come from outside the area. "We've brought in immigrants to work, because we can't get local workers," said Rick Hoffman of Seaboard.

Besides offering jobs to the communities, these hog farms also provide one more element that is not so welcome: the obnoxious odor of hog manure. Though farmers are working to eliminate this problem, people living in neighboring communities continue to complain. The factory farms pour tons of hog waste into big, smelly ponds. Earl Mitchell, who raises pigs on a small Panhandle farm, insists that pig farms do not stink if they are kept small. "We've had many friends who say they hardly smell our pigs," Mitchell said.

Besides the environmental challenges, another big impact of these megafarms is that smaller hog farmers, such as Mitchell, are quitting because they cannot afford to compete with the factory farms. Meatpackers pay less money for pigs raised on small farms—too little for the farmers to make a profit. In contrast, megafarms can raise hogs more cheaply just because of the enormous numbers of them. On the other side of the issue, they can sell the hogs for more money than small farmers are able to do. That is because meatpackers are willing to pay a little extra money because the megafarms can commit to supplying millions of pigs to them on convenient schedules.

OKLAHOMA ENERGY

Like agriculture, Oklahoma's energy industry has suffered. In the 1970s and 1980s the state's energy industry boomed—supply was low and demand was high, so prices stayed high. But even though the production of oil and natural gas is only a fourth of what it was back then, the high cost of oil in 2008 invigorated the energy industry. The demand for alternate sources of energy is creating jobs, too. "This is a fun time to be in Oklahoma," Mark

The high demand for alternate sources of energy has created many new jobs, especially in the oil industry.

Snead, a research economist at Oklahoma State University, is reported as saying. Snead was referring to the new jobs and higher salaries in the oil industry. Oil and gas are "having an important impact," Sneed added.

The economists at the Oklahoma State University William S. Spears School of Business tend to agree. While the nation's unemployment rate was rising in 2008, Oklahoma was enjoying a high rate of job growth, making the state the sixth highest in creating new jobs in the United States. At the Spears School, economists stated that Oklahoma was experiencing a "mini oil boom." In 2007 Oklahoma ranked fifth in the production of oil in the United States.

The state also produces abundant electricity. Some of this electricity is generated at the state's many dams, especially on the Arkansas and Red River systems. One of the largest dams is the Tenkiller Dam on the Illinois River. Most electricity, however, is produced by using coal and gas, which fuel the generators that create the electricity.

MINING AND MANUFACTURING

Oklahoma has large reserves of several minerals. Coal, which is used to power electricity plants, is mined in Oklahoma. The state's coal fields lie mostly in the Ozarks in the eastern areas of the state. Other mined materials include limestone, sand, gypsum, clay, feldspar, iodine, and pumice. There are salt mines, too, in the state. Every county in Oklahoma mines one type or another of mineral. Some counties mine volcanic ash.

OKLAHOMA WORKFORCE

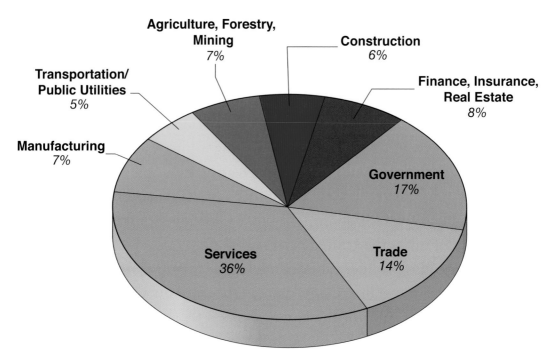

Agriculture, Forestry, Mining
7%

Construction
6%

Transportation/
Public Utilities
5%

Finance, Insurance,
Real Estate
8%

Manufacturing
7%

Government
17%

Services
36%

Trade
14%

Oklahoma's manufacturing industry contributes to the overall health of the state's economy.

Others mine iron ore. Overall, the state lists almost 750 mining sites throughout the state.

Although manufacturing is not one of Oklahoma's biggest industries, it does play a supportive role in the economy. Some of the largest manufacturing companies produce things like electronic and electrical equipment, in particular, items that foster the communications businesses. Equipment for the oil industry, such as oil pumps and pipes, is another major manufacturing enterprise. A significant aspect of the manufacturing sector is the production of airplanes and automobiles. Tires and other rubber products are also made in the state.

Some manufacturing deals with food. There are flour mills, meatpacking plants, and food-processing businesses that create products derived from milk. Other products made in the state include gypsum wallboard, or drywall (used in finishing walls in business buildings and homes), glass, and cement. There are also a few clothing manufacturers and paper mills.

Oklahoma's food-processing businesses continue to prosper.

THE SERVICE INDUSTRY

Of all the business in the state, the service industry is the most significant with reference to Oklahoma's overall economy. People at work in the service industry represent over 70 percent of the total working force.

Tourism is a big business for Oklahoma.

The service industry includes jobs in the government, including education and the military, and in the retail industry. Any organization that offers a service, whether it is a doctor's office, a hairdresser's shop, or an automobile repair shop, belongs in this category.

One of the faster growing service industries is associated with tourism. This incorporates restaurants and hotels that service tourists when they visit the state. Oklahoma City is enjoying the cash benefits of increased tourism. The city offers river cruises, museums, and of course, tours of the state capitol.

In 2008 the consensus was that Oklahoma's economy was one of the hardiest in the United States. While economic woes were affecting much of the rest of the nation, Oklahomans were realizing the benefits of high prices for oil and job growth, making the state not only a good place to visit but a great place to live. As the state moves forward, a focus on medical research and renewable energy sources is increasing, too, focusing the state's economy, as well as its citizens, on the future.

Chapter Six

A Journey to Somewhere

In some states, the attractions are concentrated in only a few places. In Oklahoma, they're spread from border to border in little hideaways that few people have heard of. It might take more than one tour of Oklahoma to see them all, but here are some spots that are "musts" to visit.

CHEROKEE COUNTRY

Northeastern Oklahoma is the most hospitable corner of the state in many ways. The land is green, rolling, and forested, and woven with lakes and streams. Its cities are the state's oldest, its history the most vivid.

Tahlequah is the capital of the Cherokee Nation. At its center is the Cherokee National Capitol, a handsome brick building completed in 1869. Near the capitol are the old Cherokee Supreme Court and the Cherokee National Prison. These buildings are as important for Cherokees as the national structures in Washington, D.C., are for all Americans. Just out of town is the Cherokee Heritage Center, where a museum and a reproduction of a seventeenth-century Cherokee village

Turner Falls Park is a popular recreation area in the Arbuckle Mountains, where families come to enjoy the beautiful scenery.

are tucked within a dark pine forest. The tribe recounts the Trail of Tears drama most summers. It brings to life the sad account of their hard migration and forced resettlement in Indian Territory.

Nearby Muscogee, one of the oldest towns in Oklahoma, today is a spirited small city, the site of the Five Civilized Tribes Museum. Besides its historical collection, the museum hosts shows of contemporary Indian art and of popular outdoor festivals where velvet ropes and glass cases don't get in between visitors and tribal culture.

To the southeast, Spiro Mounds Archaeological State Park preserves the site of a major Indian religious and ceremonial center. Archaeologists have studied a dozen mounds spread over 80 acres (32 ha) there, and have reconstructed the fantastic story of a civilization that flourished from about 800 to 1450. Not far from the mounds is Heavener Runestone State Park, where visitors may look at a large rock with eight "runes," or symbols, chiseled into its surface. The marks are undoubtedly old, but what they mean is argued about passionately. Some believe that Viking explorers carved the rune stone during a journey from Scandinavia to the heart of North America almost a thousand years ago. Others contend that the Vikings never made the trip and think the symbols were carved by Frenchmen during the early 1700s—perhaps as a practical joke. The answer to the mystery will probably never be known, but Heavener is the place to go ponder it.

Visitors come to Heavener Runestone State Park to see large rocks with symbols carved into their surface.

PLACES
TO SEE

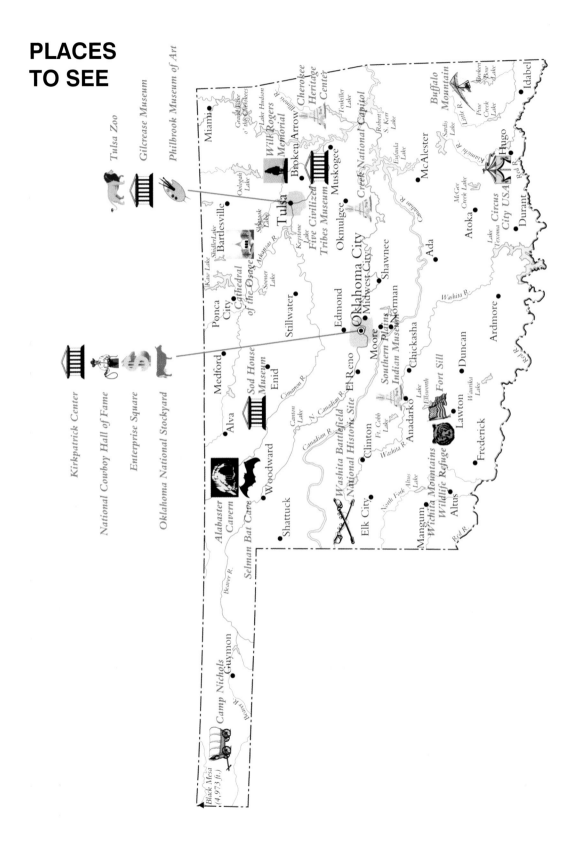

Tulsa Zoo

Gilcrease Museum

Philbrook Museum of Art

Kirkpatrick Center

National Cowboy Hall of Fame

Enterprise Square

Oklahoma National Stockyard

Alabaster Cavern

Selman Bat Cave

Black Mesa
(4,973 ft.)

Camp Nichols

Guymon

Beaver R.

Beaver R.

Shattuck

Woodward

Alva

Elk City

Mangum

Altus

North Fork Altus Lake

Red R.

Washita Battlefield National Historic Site

Clinton

Canadian R.

Washita R.

Fr. Cobb Lake

Anadarko

Wichita Mountains Wildlife Refuge

Frederick

Lawton

Waurika Lake

Fort Sill

Lake Ellsworth

Duncan

Southern Plains Indian Museum

Chickasha

El Reno

Moore

Norman

Ardmore

Red R.

Medford

Enid

Sod House Museum

Canton Lake

N. Canadian R.

Cimarron R.

Stillwater

Edmond

Oklahoma City
Midwest City

Shawnee

Ada

Atoka

Lake Texoma

Durant

Ponca City

Cathedral of the Osage

Kaw Lake

Shidler Lake

Keystone Lake

Spavinaw Lake

Bartlesville

Skiatook Lake

Arkansas R.

Tulsa

Oologah Lake

Five Civilized Tribes Museum

Okmulgee

Creek National Capitol

Okemah R.

McAlester

Eufaula Lake

Robert S. Kerr Lake

McGee Creek Lake

Circus City USA

Hugo

Hugo Lake

Canadian R.

Will Rogers Memorial

Broken Arrow

Muskogee

Grand Lake o' the Cherokees

Lake Hudson

Fort Gibson R.

Cherokee Heritage Center

Tenkiller Lake

Miami

Buffalo Mountain

Sardis Lake

Little R.

Pine Creek Lake

Broken Bow Lake

Idabel

Kiamichi R.

Red R.

The Creek National Capitol is in Okmulgee. A sober building completed in 1878, it sits on the town square. In the 1920s some Okmulgeeans thought the building looked old-fashioned and wanted to tear it down. "And what will you put in its place," asked Will Rogers, "a hotel, post office, hamburger stand, drug store?" Rogers helped save the capitol, a fact that today's Okmulgeeans appreciate. The fine old building now houses the Creek Council House, well stocked with art and artifacts for visitors to discover. "If you can't find it anywhere else, it's here," proclaimed museum director Debbie Martin. It's also the place where the tribal government holds its meetings.

And finally, Tulsa—the anchor of northeastern Oklahoma. Tulsa is "the most average city in the United States," wrote sociologist Alan Wolfe. Companies use it to field-test their advertising campaigns. It's "a perfect place to find out whether Americans will use a new mouthwash or breakfast cereal." It's also America's third-biggest petroleum city. "Every major oil company has some root in Tulsa," said industry expert Wayne Swearington.

Because of oil, Tulsa is also beautiful. While western Oklahoma suffered during the Dust Bowl years, Tulsa oil millionaires built a forest of downtown buildings in the seductive art deco style. Zigzags, streamlined curves, and flamboyant decoration expressed the builders' confidence that oil would make Tulsa a

In the world of art deco architecture, Tulsa is best known for its zigzag and streamline style.

capital of modern elegance. "No one really realizes that outside of the area," said the "first lady of Art Deco," Barbara Baer Capitman, "I have seen some of the best—absolutely best—examples of Deco buildings anywhere within a few blocks of downtown Tulsa. It's all over the city!"

LITTLE DIXIE

In Oklahoma's southeast corner, wild mountains, lakes, and farmland set off a scatter of interesting towns that remind people of the Deep South so much that the region is known as Little Dixie. Oklahomans love to camp, fish, and hike there, hoping for a glimpse of a bobcat or a flying squirrel. It's also a popular area for horseback riding and mountain biking. Buffalo Mountain has become a mecca for hang gliders. Just driving through this pretty territory on its twisting, scenic highways is a pleasure.

Below the foothills, in places like Beavers Bend State Park, the landscape turns swampy, and cypress trees drop their enormous roots into the Mountain Fork River. Visitors with expectations of high, dry plains are amazed that this is part of Oklahoma, too.

Little Dixie is where you'll find Hugo, which calls itself Circus City, USA. "We're the largest tent circus in the world," boasts Jim Royual of the Carson and Barnes Circus, one of two old-fashioned traveling shows that spend winters in Hugo. Its rare Asian elephants still provide the muscle power to raise the tents when the circus is on the road. Many circus performers settle in Hugo when they retire. Their gravestones—often carved with elephants and other circus images— dot the town's cemetery. "There's nothing left but empty popcorn sacks and wagon tracks," reads one. "The circus is gone."

Bald cypress trees can be found growing on rock islands in the middle of Mountain Fork River, as well as along the banks.

GET YOUR KICKS

Route 66 is the Mother Road of American car travel. Snaking from Chicago to Los Angeles, the highway supported strips of motels, drive-ins, and bizarre roadside attractions back in the 1940s and 1950s when these were brand-new novelties. More than 400 miles (640 km) of the storied old road wind through Oklahoma—more than in any other state.

In many places, newer highways running alongside Route 66 now attract most of the traffic and business. Some bypassed towns, such as Clinton, celebrate the old car culture with nostalgic events such as the Route 66 Festival. Other such "widespots" as Chandler seem frozen in time. The cafés, gas stations, and motels are old, rusty, often boarded-up for good. Visiting them takes you back to the days when cars had fins and whitewall tires, radios had to warm up before Elvis Presley or Chuck Berry could croon, and drivers all over the country believed that the place to "get their kicks" was on Route 66.

THE SOUTHWESTERN PLAINS

The plains of southwest Oklahoma are notable not so much for one site or another but for the landscape in which they're all contained. It's mostly flat, mostly empty, mostly space. At a glance, it looks like nothing could be concealed here—but a closer look reveals plenty of hidden treasures.

Visitors to this region will find Oklahoma's fourth-largest city, Lawton; a major army base, Fort Sill; and natural treasures such as the Wichita Mountains Wildlife Refuge. Bison, antelope, and elk share this big-skied preserve with prairie dogs and longhorn cattle. Farther northwest is the Washita Battlefield National Historic Site. The site, surrounded by the Black Kettle National Grassland, is where American general George A. Custer and eight hundred soldiers of the 7th U.S. Cavalry attacked a village in 1868, killing fifty or sixty Cheyenne Indians.

Wichita Mountains Wildlife Refuge provides habitat for large native grazing animals, such as these bison.

Anadarko is a central place on the southern plains. It's the headquarters of the Apache and Wichita tribes, and the location of the Southern Plains Indian Museum. Nearby is the National Hall of Fame for Famous American Indians, a solemn sculpture park of Indian heroes.

Anadarko's first settlers formed the Philomathic Society in order to share their experiences and escape the loneliness of frontier life. (*Philomathic* means "love of knowledge.") Thousands of items—from Indian dolls to antique medical devices—have been donated to the society over the years. These are displayed in a lively confusion of exhibits at Anadarko's Philomathic Pioneer Museum, which is housed in the old railroad station. Volun-

Anadarko's Philomathic Pioneer Museum displays relics of the past, such as this antique sculpture.

teers share the tales behind tools, costumes, photographs, and knickknacks, and will allow a careful visitor to examine them much more closely than in the average museum.

TEN LARGEST CITIES

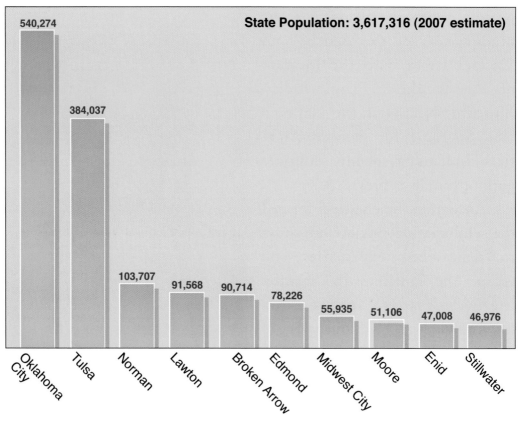

State Population: 3,617,316 (2007 estimate)

Oklahoma City 540,274
Tulsa 384,037
Norman 103,707
Lawton 91,568
Broken Arrow 90,714
Edmond 78,226
Midwest City 55,935
Moore 51,106
Enid 47,008
Stillwater 46,976

THE NORTHWEST AND THE PANHANDLE

The high, arid plains of Oklahoma's Panhandle and northwest are a "cultural boneyard," wrote environmental historian Donald Worster, "where the evidences of bad judgment and misplaced schemes lie strewn about like bleached skulls." The very first decision about where to build a town could doom everyone involved to failure. "When people wanted to settle in a town," explained one Oklahoman, "they would go to the cemetery and look at the tombstones. If there weren't many recent dates or many small children's graves, they would know that the water was safe to drink and the town was a fairly good place to live." Even today a visitor can look for such clues in the surviving towns of the western plains. A history of hard times, hard work, and fierce determination is carved into the streets and buildings and reflected in the faces of the people.

It's not hard to get the feel for those times in places like the Sod House Museum near Aline. Marshal McCully built the two-room structure in 1894 out of bricks made from turf cut from the prairie. The interior is lined with sheets to keep the constant shower of dirt and bugs out of occupants' eyes. Most homesteaders abandoned their sod houses as soon as they could afford a "real" house, which makes the McCully place a rarely seen relic. Sod houses could actually be quite comfortable—their thick walls kept them warm in the winter and cool in the fierce summer heat. The museum features antique farm machinery and a blacksmith shop.

Thousands of people once dotted the prairies of Oklahoma, but only this sod house built in 1894 by Marshal McCully remains.

The Oklahoma Panhandle used to be called No Man's Land because it wasn't part of any territory or state. This strip of dry, high land was finally assigned to Oklahoma, though the Panhandle still retains its own, distinctive style.

Near Boise City, at the very western tip of the Panhandle, is old Fort Nichols. In the nineteenth century the fort served as a way station, a travelers' place to rest, along the Santa Fe Trail—an important route for travelers going from Missouri to New Mexico. The worn ruts caused by covered wagons can still be seen on the landscape. Also visible are messages that the early wayfarers carved on the stones in the area. Many left their names and the date that they passed through.

Once the railroad was built, however, travel by covered wagons became markedly less efficient, so the fort was abandoned. Fort Nichols, however, is a good place to visit to enjoy a glimpse of a life now gone.

COW CHIP CAPITAL OF THE WORLD

One Panhandle town, Beaver, holds a festival every April that some people might avoid but others will find fascinating: the World Cow Chip Throwing Contest. In earlier days, pioneers in this nearly treeless area would gather cow manure for fuel, tossing the dried chips into their wagons as they worked. Today, people come from all over the country every April to sling the dung competitively. Most contestants claim to know the secret for success in this obscure sport. Ron Speer hunts for chips from cows who eat buffalo grass; they stick together well, he said.

Nearly everyone enjoys the annual joke, but others, such as rancher Lloyd Barby, aren't inclined to compete. "I never throwed any," he explained, "because I walked in it all my life."

ARNETT IN SUMMER

Oklahoma poet Patrick Worth Gray captured the scorched landscape of western Oklahoma in one of the many poems he set in the northwest town of Arnett.

> Another Oklahoma town
> Hunkered down by a dry wash
> Cracked by drought in summer
> Heatwaves worming up from its convulsions.
> The black, sticky streets slither
> Like snakes, our car rattles,
> We shrink from the heat as though
> It is coiled. The dry air
> Crackles in our nostrils. We park
> And watch phantoms shimmer.

SMACK-DAB IN THE MIDDLE

Will Rogers once boasted that "Oklahoma is the heart, it's the vital organ of our national existence." At the heart of the heart is Oklahoma City, smack-dab in the middle of the state. Oklahoma's largest city was "born grown"—its population went from zero to thousands in a few hours during the first land rush on April 22, 1889. After more than a century, the capital still has some of the most fascinating features of any place in the state.

Many of Oklahoma City's attractions are designed for kids. The Kirkpatrick Center is a collection of seven "kid-friendly" museums devoted to science, art, Indians, and photography. The National Cowboy & Western Heritage Museum hosts the Chuck Wagon Gathering and Children's Cowboy Festival every May. Then there's Enterprise Square, a museum that celebrates American business. Visitors can learn about successful businesspeople and how they succeeded and hear singing dollar bills praise the virtues of economic competition.

The Kirkpatrick Center is an outstanding seven-museum complex, which includes a planetarium, greenhouse, and aerospace museum with laser lightshows.

Elsewhere in Oklahoma City you might want to visit Stockyards City, the neighborhood that grew around the country's largest cattle auction operation. You can watch the animals parade into the auction ring and listen to the frenzied loud singsong of the auctioneers, then visit the western wear clothing stores and antique shops around the corner.

Many newcomers are struck by the small-town homeyness of Oklahoma's largest city. "Clerks take time to say hello. It's not a 'keep your nose to the grindstone' attitude," said newcomer Jane Morilak. Friends and family don't necessarily understand her

Many who visit Stockyards City, come to see Oklahoma cowboys working the livestock.

love affair with her adopted city. "Our daughter keeps sending us towels with cactuses on them," laughed Morilak. "She thinks we're living in the desert."

Misconceptions such as this often cloud outsiders' mental pictures of Oklahoma. Most visitors see just a little and leave not quite understanding the place. Misleading images abound: land rushes, deserts, Dust Bowls, terrorist bombings. It takes more work to figure out what Oklahoma really is. Read more books. Or better yet, visit Oklahoma yourself!

THE FLAG: The Oklahoma flag shows an Osage warrior's shield against a blue background. Two symbols of peace—an olive branch and a peace pipe—cross the shield. The flag was adopted in 1925.

THE SEAL: The state seal, which was adopted in 1907, displays a white star. In its center, a frontiersman and an Indian shake hands, symbolizing cooperation among the people of Oklahoma. The star's five points contain the symbols of the Cherokee, Choctaw, Chickasaw, Seminole, and Creek nations, five tribes that settled in Oklahoma. Around the star are arrayed forty-five stars, representing the states in the Union when Oklahoma became the forty-sixth.

State Survey

Statehood: November 16, 1907

Origin of Name: From the Choctaw words *ukla*, meaning "person," and *huma*, meaning "red"

Nickname: Sooner State, Boomer's Paradise

Capital: Oklahoma City

Motto: Labor Conquers All Things

Bird: Scissor-tailed flycatcher

Flower: Mistletoe

Tree: Redbud

Animal: Bison

Fish: White or sand bass

Grass: Indian grass

Reptile: Mountain boomer collared lizard

Scissor-tailed flycatcher

Mistletoe

OKLAHOMA

The 1942 Broadway musical *Oklahoma!*, with lyrics by Oscar Hammerstein II and music by Richard Rogers, has remained one of the most popular shows ever produced. It was based on the play *Green Grow the Lilacs* by Lynn Riggs and tells the story of the conflicts between the cowboys and the farmers in late-nineteenth-century Oklahoma Territory. This song was one of the many hits from the show. It was adopted by the Oklahoma legislature as the official state song in 1953.

Words by Oscar Hammerstein 2nd

Music by Richard Rogers

Rock: Barite rose rock

Wildflower: Indian blanket

Country-and-Western Song: "Faded Love," by Bob Wills and John Willis

GEOGRAPHY

Highest Point: 4,973 feet (1,515 m) above sea level, at Black Mesa

Lowest Point: 287 feet (90 m) above sea level, along the Little River in McCurtain County

Area: 69,903 square miles (181,000 square km)

Greatest Distance, North to South: 231 miles (370 km)

Greatest Distance, East to West: 478 miles (770 km)

Bordering States: Colorado and Kansas to the north, Missouri and Arkansas to the east, Texas to the south, New Mexico to the west

Hottest Recorded Temperature: 120 °F (50 °C) at Alva on July 18, 1936; at Altus on July 19, 1936, and August 12, 1936; at Poteau on August 10, 1936, and at Tishomingo on July 26, 1934

Coldest Recorded Temperature: –27 °F (–30 °C) at Vinita on February 13, 1905, and at Watts on January 18, 1930

Average Annual Precipitation: 33 inches (84 cm)

Major Rivers: Arkansas, Beaver, Blue, Canadian, Chikaskia, Cimarron, Kiamichi, Little, Mountain Fork, Neosho, Poteau, Red, Salt Fork, Verdigris, Washita

Major Lakes: Atoka, Broken Bow, Eufala, Fort Gibson, Foss, Great Salt Plains, Kaw, Lake o' the Cherokees, Oologah, Pine Creek, Sardis, Tenkiller, Texoma, Thunderbird, Waurika

Trees: ash, cedar, cottonwood, elm, hickory, maple, pecan, pine, sweet gum, walnut

Wild Plants: bluestem, buffalo grass, dogwood, goldenrod, Indian grass, mesquite, petunia, primrose, sagebrush, sunflower, verbena, violet, wild indigo

Animals: armadillo, bat, coyote, deer, elk, gray fox, mink, opossum, otter, prairie dog, rabbit, raccoon, red fox, squirrel

Birds: blue jay, cardinal, crow, dove, duck, meadowlark, mockingbird, oriole, owl, roadrunner, robin, sparrow, thrush

Fish: bass, buffalo fish, carp, catfish, crappie, drumfish, paddlefish, sunfish

Endangered Animals: American burying beetle, black-capped vireo, Eskimo curlew, gray bat, Indiana bat, least tern, Ouachita rock pocketbook, Ozark big-eared bat, red-cockaded woodpecker, whooping crane

Prairie dog

TIMELINE

Oklahoma History

c. 1200 C.E. The Spiro people build huge mounds in what is now eastern Oklahoma.

1500s Many Indian tribes, including the Arapaho, Caddo, Kiowa, Osage, Pawnee, and Wichita, live in present-day Oklahoma.

1541 A party led by Spaniard Francisco Vásquez de Coronado crosses Oklahoma while searching for gold, becoming the first Europeans to set foot in the region.

1682 France claims Oklahoma.

1714 Juchereau de St. Denis becomes the first Frenchman to set foot in Oklahoma.

1762 France cedes Louisiana, which includes Oklahoma, to Spain.

1800 Spain cedes Louisiana back to France.

1803 Most of Oklahoma becomes U.S. territory as part of the Louisiana Purchase.

1824 Forts Gibson and Towson, the region's first military posts, are built.

1825 Much of Oklahoma is designated Indian Territory and is set aside for Indians.

1830–42 Thousands of Cherokee, Choctaw, Chickasaw, Creek, and Seminole Indians are forced into Oklahoma from their homes in the southeast.

1844 The *Cherokee Advocate*, Oklahoma's first newspaper, begins publishing in Tahlequah.

1861–65 Many people in Indian Territory support the Confederacy during the Civil War.

1867 Texas cowboys make the first great cattle drive up the Chisholm Trail across Oklahoma to stockyards in Kansas.

1872 The Missouri-Kansas-Texas Railroad, the first railroad across present-day Oklahoma, is completed.

1889 Parts of Oklahoma are opened to white settlement; on April 22, 50,000 people move to Oklahoma in its first land rush.

1890 The Territory of Oklahoma is established; Oklahoma State University is founded.

1897 Oklahoma's first significant oil well is drilled near Bartlesville.

1907 Oklahoma becomes the forty-sixth state; the state prohibits the sale of alcohol.

1910 Oklahoma City becomes the state capital.

1921 As many as three hundred African Americans are killed in Tulsa in one of the nation's worst incidents of racial violence.

1928 The vast Oklahoma City oil field is opened.

1930s In what is known as the Dust Bowl, severe drought and high winds cause massive dust storms, forcing hundreds of thousands of people to leave the state.

1941–45 The United States participates in World War II.

1959 The state's prohibition of alcohol is repealed.

1970 The Arkansas River Navigation System is completed, allowing barges to travel all the way to Tulsa from the Gulf of Mexico.

1982 Oklahoma suffers as oil prices decline drastically.

1990 Oklahoma becomes the first state to limit the number of terms its state legislators may serve.

1995 A terrorist bomb blows up a federal office building in Oklahoma City, killing 168 people.

2001 The Oklahoma state legislature passes the 1921 Tulsa Race Riot Reconciliation Act.

2007 Oklahoma celebrates its centennial.

ECONOMY

Agricultural Products: beef cattle, biofuels (i.e., switchgrass) catfish, chickens, corn, cotton, eggs, hay, hogs, milk, peaches, peanuts, pecans, sorghum, soybeans, turkeys, wheat

Manufactured Products: aircraft equipment, electronic components, food products, machinery, metal products, television parts, tires

Natural Resources: coal, crushed stone, iodine, natural gas, oil, sand, gypsum, gravel

Business and Trade: banking, insurance, real estate, wholesale and retail trade

Soybeans

CALENDAR OF CELEBRATIONS

International Finals Rodeo Before watching the dust fly as some of the world's best cowboys compete in bull riding, steer wrestling, and other competitions, check out the huge parade of horses, wagons, and musicians that opens this January rodeo in Oklahoma City.

Bitter Creek Frontier Daze People dressed as outlaws, sheriffs, cowboys, and soldiers depict life in nineteenth-century Oklahoma during this festival near Watonga each February.

Weatherford World Championship Hog Calling Contest Each spring, hog callers from around the world travel to the small town of Weatherford to show off their best oinks and soo-wees. Afterward, they can eat their fill of barbecue.

Azalea Festival At this April festival in Muscogee, visitors can admire 40 acres (16 ha) of brightly blooming azaleas.

Azalea Festival

Red Earth Cultural Festival

This June event in Oklahoma City calls itself the World's Biggest Powwow. Members of more than a hundred different tribes participate in the dancing competitions and exhibitions. Visitors also enjoy parades, art shows, and lots of delicious food.

Red Earth Cultural Festival

Pecan Festival Five million pounds of pecans are harvested in Okmulgee County each year. In June the town of Okmulgee honors its favorite nut with a festival that has produced the world's largest pecan pie, largest pecan cookie, and largest pecan brownie.

Kiamichi Owa Chito Festival of the Forest Outdoor events such as canoe racing and chainsaw carving are the big draws at this June extravaganza in Beavers Bend Resort Park.

Ada Air Expo At this July festival in Ada, people take to the sky any way they can. Some are in hot air balloons, others are in airplanes, and still others are wafting to the ground with parachutes.

Cherokee National Holiday Besides a powwow, arts and crafts displays and workshops, this September event in Tahlequah includes the state of the nation speech by the principal chief of the Cherokee Nation.

Watonga Cheese Festival Each October Watonga is the site of cheese tastings, historical reenactments, and an art show.

Chickasha Festival of Light During the Christmas season millions of lights give Chickasha a festive feeling.

STATE STARS

Troy Aikman (1966–   ) was one of the leading quarterbacks in the National Football League. An extraordinary passer, he led the Dallas Cowboys to three Super Bowl victories in four years. Aikman was born in California and spent much of his youth in Henryetta, Oklahoma.

Johnny Bench (1947–   ), one of baseball's best catchers, was born in Oklahoma City. He earned the National League Rookie of the Year Award in 1968. An excellent defensive player, Bench won ten consecutive Gold Glove awards. He was also a big offensive threat, leading the league in home runs twice and in runs batted in three times. Bench helped the Cincinnati Reds win the World Series in 1975 and 1976. He was elected to the National Baseball Hall of Fame in 1989.

Garth Brooks (1962–   ) is one of the world's most popular country singers. His 1991 album, *Ropin' the Wind,* was the first country album to reach number one on the pop charts the week it came out. Brooks, who is famous for his energetic live shows, is one of the best-selling acts in music history. He has had more than twenty number-one hits, including "Friends in Low Places" and "Rodeo." Brooks was born in Tulsa.

Garth Brooks

Charlie Christian (1916–1942) was an influential jazz electric guitarist. Christian played sophisticated music on his guitar, performing solos that were more like what horn players usually played. His style and improvisations influenced jazz guitarists for decades. Christian grew up in Oklahoma City.

Ralph Ellison (1914–1994), a native of Oklahoma City, wrote *Invisible Man*, which is generally considered one of the greatest American novels of the twentieth century. The novel describes a young black man's travels as he searches for his identity and for acceptance. The man comes to realize that, as an African American, he is ignored—he's invisible to society. Both brutal and honest, realistic and dreamlike, *Invisible Man* earned Ellison the National Book Award in 1953. Ralph Ellison, who also published essays and short stories to great acclaim, was awarded the Medal of Freedom, the nation's highest civilian honor, in 1969.

Ralph Ellison

Woody Guthrie (1912–1967), a native of Okemah, was an influential folk singer. As a sixteen-year-old, Guthrie left home to play guitar with a traveling magic show. He ended up in California, where he often performed at migrant labor camps. Guthrie eventually published more than a thousand songs, often about people facing hard times. His most famous is probably "This Land Is Your Land." Guthrie's autobiography, *Bound for Glory*, is a classic tale of life during the Great Depression.

Tony Hillerman (1925–2008), one of the nation's most successful mystery writers, was born in Sacred Heart and attended the University of Oklahoma. Later, he moved to New Mexico, where he became fascinated by Navajo Indian culture. His novels, such as *Skinwalkers* and *The Thief of Time*, are both exciting mysteries and careful examinations of Navajo traditions and contemporary life.

Allan Houser (1914–1994) was a leading sculptor who propelled American-Indian sculpture into modern directions. A Chiracahua Apache, Houser depicted traditional Indians such as warriors in a variety of materials, including bronze, steel, stone, and alabaster. In 1992 he became the first Indian to receive the National Medal of the Arts, the nation's highest award for artistic achievement. Houser was born in Apache.

Karl Jansky (1905–1950), who was born in Norman, founded radio astronomy—the study of distant objects by the radio waves they emit. An electrical engineer, Jansky was trying to reduce the static that often interrupted long-distance radio transmissions. In 1932 he discovered that the steady hiss was the result of radio waves that seemed to come from the center of the galaxy. Previously it was thought that all radio waves were produced by people. In recognition of his contribution, today the unit used to measure the intensity of radio waves is called the jansky.

Doc Holliday (1851–1887), who was born in Griffin, was a legendary gambler and gunfighter. He worked as a dentist in the East but moved west in 1872 because the dry climate was supposed to be better for his ailing lungs. There, his gunfighting became legendary. In 1881 he was involved in the famous gunfight at the O.K. Corral.

William Wayne Keeler (1908–1987) was both a chief of the Cherokee Nation and the chief executive officer of Phillips Petroleum. Keller spent his entire career with Phillips Petroleum, working his way up to become president and CEO in 1967, positions he held until he retired in 1987. After he became the Cherokee chief in 1949, he founded the first Cherokee National Holiday and organized the Cherokee National Historical Society. He also helped the Cherokee win back land that had been taken from them by the U.S. government. Keeler grew up in Bartlesville.

Shannon Lucid (1943–   ), is a biochemist and an astronaut who grew up in Bethany and holds the American record for the longest stay in space. Lucid attended the University of Oklahoma. She had already been on four space missions when the space shuttle *Atlantis* brought her to the Russian *Mir* space station in 1996. Lucid stayed on *Mir* for 188 days and four hours—longer than any other American has spent in space.

Shannon Lucid

Wilma Mankiller (1945–   ), who was born in Stilwell, was the first female principal chief of the Cherokee Nation. After becoming chief in 1985, Mankiller worked to improve health care and education and fostered many community self-help programs. Under her leadership, the number of members in the tribe tripled.

Mickey Mantle (1931–1995), a native of Spavinaw who grew up in Commerce, was one of baseball's greatest hitters. He played centerfield for the New York Yankees for eighteen years, helping them win seven World Series. A great switch hitter, Mantle ranks eighth in career home runs with 536. This three-time American League Most Valuable Player had his best year in 1956, when he led the league in home runs, runs batted in, and batting average. Mantle was elected to the National Baseball Hall of Fame in 1974.

Mickey Mantle

Reba McEntire (1955–   ) is one of the nation's most popular country singers. With her great range and a voice that can be both velvety and sassy, she has hit number one on the charts many times with songs such as "How Blue" and "Somebody Should Leave." McEntire was born in Chockie.

N. Scott Momaday (1934–), a member of the Kiowa tribe, became the first American Indian to win the Pulitzer Prize for fiction when his book *House Made of Dawn* was awarded the honor in 1969. The novel is the story of a World War II veteran who is struggling to find his place in both the Indian and non-Indian worlds. Some of Momaday's other works, such as *The Way to Rainy Mountain*, have retold Kiowa legends. Momaday was born in Lawton.

N. Scott Momaday

Frank Phillips (1873–1950) moved to Bartlesville in 1903 from his home in Iowa to drill for oil. In 1917 he founded Phillips Petroleum Company, which grew into one of the nation's largest oil companies.

Will Rogers (1879–1935) was one of the most popular entertainers of the early twentieth century. Born in Oologah, he began his career as a trick roper in Wild West shows before moving on to vaudeville. He eventually became a tremendously popular radio personality and newspaper columnist, famous for his gentle, folksy humor. Rogers also appeared in more than seventy films, including *State Fair*, *Life Begins at Forty*, and *Judge Priest*.

Will Rogers

Maria Tallchief (1925–   ) was one of first American ballerinas to gain international acclaim. Famed for her technical precision, subtlety, and emotion, she was the prima ballerina of the New York City Ballet from 1947 to 1960. She is perhaps best remembered for her performance as the Sugar Plum Fairy in *The Nutcracker*. After her retirement in 1965, Tallchief turned her attention to teaching. In 1979 she founded the Chicago City Ballet. Tallchief, who is half Osage, was born in Fairfax.

Maria Tallchief

Jim Thorpe (1887–1953), a Sac and Fox Indian from Prague, is considered the greatest athlete of the first half of the twentieth century. At the 1912 Olympics he dominated the track and field competition, winning the gold medal in both the pentathlon and the decathlon. But the following year, he was stripped of his medals because he had played semiprofessional baseball when he was younger. At the time Olympics only allowed amateur athletes. Thorpe later became a professional baseball and football player. In 1920 he became the president of the American Professional Football Association, which would become the National Football League. Many years after Thorpe's death, the International Olympic Committee gave duplicate gold medals to his children, realizing they should never have been taken away.

Alfre Woodard (1953–) is an acclaimed actress, renowned for her consistently strong, controlled performances. Woodard has a remarkable range, playing funny, wise, wary, and every other state with equal skill. She has appeared in such films as *Passion Fish*, *Crooklyn*, and *Bopha!*. She has also won Emmy Awards for her performances in the television series *Hill Street Blues* and *L.A. Law*. Woodard was born in Tulsa.

Alfre Woodard

TOUR THE STATE

Cherokee Heritage Center (Tahlequah) At this site you can tour a replica of a seventeenth-century Cherokee village and see a play about the disastrous Trail of Tears. You can also watch demonstrations of soap making, weaving, and other traditional skills.

Will Rogers Memorial (Claremore) A large statue of the famous entertainer graces the town that Rogers called home.

Tenkiller State Park (Vian) Hiking, fishing, camping, scuba diving—this park is the perfect place to enjoy the outdoors.

Talimena Scenic Byway (Talihina) Sharp curves and stunning vistas dot this tour of the Ouachita National Forest. In the spring wildflowers and dogwood blooms color the roadside, while in the fall the brilliant golds and rusts of the changing leaves take over.

Talimena Scenic Byway

Gilcrease Museum (Tulsa) One of the nation's best collections of western art, this museum contains everything from Indian art made more than a thousand years ago to works by such renowned western artists as George Catlin.

Tulsa Zoo (Tulsa) A highlight of this zoo is the rain forest exhibit, where colorful birds flit around your head while lizards and other creatures move among the lush plants.

Philbrook Museum of Art (Tulsa) After checking out the wide-ranging art housed in this beautiful mansion, many visitors enjoy strolling through its gardens past sparkling ponds.

Philbrook Museum of Art

Mac's Antique Car Museum (Tulsa) Fifty-one carefully restored cars are on exhibit at this museum, including a 1912 Model T.

Tallgrass Prairie Preserve (Pawhuska) Buffalo roam this preserve, where some grasses grow 8 feet (2 m) high. You might also spy bobcats and beavers, antelope and armadillos.

Cathedral of the Osage (Pawhuska) Many of the exquisite stained glass windows of this church depict American Indians.

Tallgrass Prairie Preserve

Oklahoma History Center (Oklahoma City) At this museum visitors can see all sorts of artifacts of Oklahoma's history including a real buffalo-hide tepee, a wagon that was used in the land rush, and many oil-drilling tools.

Oklahoma History Center

Science Museum of Oklahoma (Oklahoma City) You can climb inside a molecule, tour a human body, figure out what causes lightning, or try out hundreds of other interactive exhibits at this fascinating museum.

Oklahoma National Stockyards (Oklahoma City) Listen to the rapid-fire auctions and watch the cowboys on horseback manage the cattle at the center of the Oklahoma cattle industry.

National Cowboy & Western Heritage Museum (Oklahoma City) All aspects of the West, not just cowboys, are honored at this museum. You'll see exhibits on American Indians, rodeos, and movie Westerns. You can even explore a replica of a frontier town.

National Cowboy & Western Heritage Museum

Southern Plains Indian Museum (Anadarko) Outstanding traditional arts and contemporary crafts are on display at this museum.

Wichita Mountains Wildlife Refuge (Holy City) Elk, bison, bobcats, and even longhorn cattle make their home in the nation's oldest managed wildlife preserve.

Fort Sill (Lawton) This fort, founded in 1869, abounds with history. You can see the guardhouse where the great Apache warrior Geronimo was held prisoner, as well as displays on Quanah Parker, the last Comanche leader to remain free. Also on the grounds is the cemetery where Geronimo, Parker, and many other famous Indians are buried.

Fort Sill

Alabaster Caverns State Park

Alabaster Caverns State Park (Freedom) Visitors who hike deep into
the colorful caverns will see all sorts of crystals and minerals, but the
highlight is the beautiful black alabaster, which is found in only two
other caves in the world.

Little Sahara State Park

Little Sahara State Park (Waynoka) Crowds of dune buggies and motorcycles greet visitors at this park, where hundreds of acres of rideable sand dunes shift as the strong wind blows.

Selman Bat Cave (Freedom) Most evenings in July and August, you can watch a million Mexican free-tailed bats head out from this cave for a night of feasting on insects. They eat about 10 tons of insects every night.

Black Mesa State Park and Nature Preserve (Kenton) A hike to
Oklahoma's highest point offers an extraordinary view of the
Panhandle and beyond. Before you head up, make sure you stop to
look at the dinosaur tracks.

Black Mesa State Park and Nature Preserve

FUN FACTS

Oklahoma is called the Sooner State because some of the settlers in the first land rush in 1889 jumped the gun. They snuck out early to stake their claims, getting to the prime land "sooner" than they should have.

The city of Guthrie was the first state capitol of Oklahoma.

The world's first parking meter was installed in Oklahoma City on July 16, 1935.

The name Oklahoma comes from the Choctaw language and is translated as a "red person."

Oklahoma City was also the site of the first shopping cart. Grocery store owner Sylvan Goldman noticed that customers were having trouble carrying baskets and watching their children, so he came up with the idea of basket carriers on wheels. No one used them until he hired people to push them around the store so other folks would see how useful they were.

FIND OUT MORE

Books and websites can all take you further into Oklahoma. Here are some suggestions for starting that journey.

GENERAL STATE BOOKS

Brown, Jonathan A. *Oklahoma.* Strongsville, OH: Gareth Stevens Publishing, 2005.

Dorman, Robert L. *It Happened in Oklahoma.* Guilford, CT: TwoDot, 2006.

SPECIAL INTEREST BOOKS

Alexander, M. J. *Salt of the Red Earth: A Century of Wit and Wisdom from Oklahoma's Elders.* Oklahoma City: Oklahoma Heritage Association, 2007.

Hardeman, Michael. *Oklahoma Wonder and Light.* Johnson City, TN: Mountain Trail Press, 2007.

Lassek, P. J. *Oklahoma Curiosities: Quirky Characters, Roadside Oddities & Other Offbeat Stuff.* Guilford, CT: Globe Pequot, 2008.

Simermeyer, Genevieve. *Meet Christopher: An Osage Indian Boy from Oklahoma.* Tulsa, OK: Council Oak Books, 2008.

FICTION

Krueger, Kathryn L. *Road to Grandma's House.* Outskirts Press, 2005

WEBSITES

Website of the *Daily Oklahoman*

www.oklahoman.com

Oklahoma's leading newspaper. Besides offering the day's news, this site has great links to other Oklahoma websites, including some designed by and for children.

State's Official Website

www.oklaosf.state.ok.us

Go there to learn about the government and the economy and to find links to lots more Oklahoma websites.

Index

Page numbers in **boldface** are illustrations and charts.

ABOUT THE AUTHORS

Guy Baldwin is a writer who lives in New York City. He has fond memories of visits to Oklahoma over the last two decades and especially appreciates Oklahoma's quirky variety of land and people.

Joyce Hart is a freelance writer who has written and coauthored several books about the states. She has traveled through Oklahoma three times, once to attend summer powwows. She lives in Washington State and completed her research for this book at the library on the Port Madison Indian reservation, home of the Suquamish tribe of Chief Seattle.